Weather the Storm

By Taylor Birch

To Kevin Birch,

who helps me see the big picture when I get stuck in my head.

Table of Contents

"However dark conditions may seem in this world today, whatever the storms we are facing personally... joy can be ours now."

- Russell M. Nelson

Introduction

In the summer of 2019, I had an out-of-body experience that left me pleading to come back to earth. I was surrounded by exquisite pastel colors—more vivid and wide-ranging than anything I had ever seen. I was also enveloped by intense peace and joy. However, floating between this life and the next, my heart was rent in two. I couldn't stand the thought of leaving my wife, JoAnne.

When the experience ended, I found myself in bed. As I became aware of my body, I was overcome with waves of pain. It was as if that brief time away had erased decades of physical suffering, only to have it all come crashing back at once. Although I experience a certain agony daily, it is worth it to be here with her.

That experience properly motivated me to make a record of my life with the hope that my story will help others sustain their faith through the storms of life.

Part One

Trauma

When people ask, "What happened to you?" I often jokingly reply, "I was hit by a truck," which always gets a chuckle, but it is the truth.

It happened my freshman year of high school. It was the year my football team won Districts; the season I didn't finish. At the time, we lived in a town called Toppenish located on the Yakima Indian Reservation in eastern Washington. After school, my friend Mark and I rode bikes around town. As evening approached, he asked me to ride with him halfway home. He lived six miles away in Wapato. Mark went to the same church as I did, but his family didn't attend most Sundays. To be completely honest, he was somewhat of a wild child. Despite his wild streak, we were fast friends. Together, we rode bikes around town with our long Beatles hair flowing in the wind.

We rode to my house and I ran inside. I took a quick left through the family room and ran back to the kitchen where my mom could typically be found cooking or cleaning. She wasn't there. "Hey mom?" I walked back through the house and found her standing by the piano in the living room. Always a classy dresser, my mom was wearing a nice blouse, and slacks with a zipper up the left side. Out of breath, I panted, "I'm going to ride with Mark halfway home. I'll be right back."

She replied, "No, Martin. I don't have a good feeling about that highway. I don't want you to go."

"I already told him I'd go halfway with him."

Before she could reply, I was already back outside. I grabbed my ten-speed and left a trail of dust behind me. A few minutes later I reached the two-lane highway with Mark close behind me.

A short way up the road, I heard him yell out, "Switch!"

Confused, I turned my head and called back, "Switch? What do you mean, switch?"

He yelled that as cars came up behind us, we would cross to the left side of the highway so they could stay in their lane as they passed us. After the cars went by, we would switch back to the right side. I had never done that before, but it sounded reasonable enough. By the time he explained the switching process, the car had already passed. "We'll do it on the next one," he yelled as we continued to pedal.

I readied myself. I was prepared when Mark called out again, "Switch!"

This time I knew what to do. I leaned hard to the left and swerved into the middle of the highway. My heart raced as I pedaled faster. I was over the center line when Mark hollered, "No, no! Switch back!" His voice reached an octave higher than I had ever heard it before. My stomach sunk as if anticipating a blow.

I crouched down over the bike and started to steer back to the right. I was barely over the dashed white lines when I checked to see how close the car was. As I turned my head to the right, I was blindsided by the passenger rear-view mirror of a large flatbed truck. There was a flash of white, then black.

...

I opened my eyes. The impact had knocked me off my bike. I laid on the road staring up into the darkened sky. My face was wet and warm. I could not see my bike anywhere.

Soon, Mark was at my side yelling at the guy in the truck. Slowly, the words started to make sense, "Go call for an ambulance!" he hollered again and again. Those were the days before cell phones, when calling for an ambulance meant finding someone home who would let you use their phone.

I felt stuck in limbo between a dream and reality. *What happened? Am I going to die? My mom is going to kill me...* Mark knelt beside me and helped me remove my shirt. He held it to my gushing face. It was immediately soaked through, turning the cotton sticky, dark and useless.

Thankfully, Mark got a car to stop. Unbelievably, I was able to get up and limp my way to the car. Once in the seat, I slipped into darkness.

...

I was laying on an operating table. The sharp smell of disinfectant filled my nostrils. When I opened my eyes, it felt like I was looking through a kaleidoscope. The hospital lights refracted off the glass in my eyes and turned everything technicolor. Numerous hospital staff surrounded my head. They pulled shards of glass out of my face and added stitches. Although there was a large cut through my right eyelid, my eyes were not significantly damaged.

Before long, both of my parents were there. We learned I had four crushed vertebrae in my lower back and my left leg had been run over. The doctors told us that I had lost a substantial amount of blood. Had I waited for an ambulance, I would not have survived. Those words laid heavily on my heart. I was tired, confused, and honestly, scared.

My parents called someone from our church to come out and give me a priesthood blessing. As we waited for him to arrive, I vowed to God, "Lord, if I live, I will go and serve You on a mission." Up until that night I had been ambivalent about serving a mission, but I determined then that if God would spare my life, I would spend the rest of it serving Him in whatever way I could.

When Blake Lott arrived, the look on his face said it all. I was pretty messed up. He gently placed his hands on my head and told me in the blessing that I would be okay. He also said I would not have any noticeable facial scars, which at the time seemed impossible because I ended up with hundreds of stitches on the right side of my face. I mean, I looked like I went through a meat grinder. So much for dating, right?

My older sister, Kaelin, who was studying to become a medical technician, came to see me. Kaelin was so upset by my battered face that she got in an accident and nearly totaled my parents' car two blocks from the hospital.

I later learned that the man who drove me to the hospital, the one who saved my life, reupholstered his car because my blood had soaked into everything. I was lucky to be alive.

. . .

Shortly after getting out of the hospital, I returned to school. The doctors warned me to be careful as my body continued to recover from the accident and, for the most part, I was. I dropped out of football for the rest of the year and limited my other activities.

I didn't want to baby myself. So, sometimes during lunch I would play basketball. There were a few of us, guys and girls, who would play together. One afternoon things got out of hand. The game started out alright, but before long people started playing rough. They were jockeying for the ball and before I knew it, I had been tackled to the ground and felt a sharp pain in my lower back. I didn't want my classmates to see I was hurt, so I slowly got up from the ground, set my face to stone and hobbled toward my dad's classroom. He taught English in the room next to my last period class. By the time I got there, lunch was over, and I went to my class instead.

The rest of the day went by in a blur. I remember the teacher left the room for a time. While he was gone, I laid down on the floor with my feet up against the wall to relieve the pressure on my back. This was met by general teasing from the kids in the room. When the teacher returned, he asked what I was doing on the floor. I opened my eyes momentarily and said, "My back is killing me. Please just let me lie here."

Not too long afterward, the last bell rang for the day. I struggled to get to my feet and took baby steps through the hallway toward my dad's door. I stood in the doorway and met his gaze from across the room.

Holding back tears, I said, "Dad, hey...my back." He rushed to my side and insisted we go to the hospital.

Little did we know the effect this accident would have on the rest of my life. It was like tapping the first domino; it set everything else into motion.

Life Before the Diagnosis

My mom grew up in a farmhouse in southeast Idaho. Her family owned over one thousand-acres of land used mainly for raising beef cattle. At fifteen, she and her younger sister, Sydney, spent the weekdays away from home. They stayed in a small, two-room ranch house located on the property about an hour north of Soda Springs in a place called Grays Lake. The girls were responsible for feeding all the men hired as ranch hands during the week. They chopped lumber to feed the wood burning stove and made three square meals a day from scratch for a large group of hungry men.

Sometimes, the evenings were so cold they chased mice out of their beds before laying down. Every weekend they drove the old truck back home to reload supplies. It was a lot of responsibility at such a tender age, but they didn't mind. In fact, my mom preferred being away from the drama of the house.

She left Grace, Idaho after high school graduation to pursue a nursing degree at Utah State University. It was there she met my father, a handsome man with cropped hair and a wide smile. Shortly thereafter, they were married in the Idaho Falls temple.

Unfortunately, after only two years she was forced by her declining health to withdraw from school entirely. She did not yet know that the next decade would be filled with exploratory surgeries searching for answers to her failing health. The doctors eventually found the root of her problem, and the cause was genetic.

In the years that followed, my dad went on to finish his degree and become a teacher. He also took on consulting work with local fruit farmers to provide for our growing family which, by their sixth anniversary, had grown to include three children: Kirk, Kaelin and myself.

. . .

Due to her poor health, my mom couldn't always look after me, so I often went with my dad to work in the fields. That is how I found myself driving a pickup at seven years old.

As part of his consulting work, my dad ran lines— long lengths of one-inch PVC pipes—down the fields. He dammed up the irrigation ditches and dipped each of the hundreds of pipes into the pools to supply water to crops further away. By stretching my foot out to reach the brake and positioning myself to nearly standing, I could just see over the steering wheel. I let the truck idle down the dirt road like that for hours.

After we crossed the entire length of the farm, my dad got in the truck and drove us home. It wasn't long before I was driving tractors, potato trucks and all sorts of machinery on the farm. That time with my dad instilled in me a desire and love for farm work. Before long, I was moving water lines myself.

...

As a young boy of twelve, I spent the summer in Idaho working alongside my cousin Peter. We moved water lines on different farms. With my mom's health the way it was, it gave my parents a break while simultaneously providing me with an opportunity to earn some money and make memories with my cousins. Peter was two years older than me, but we had always been close. It was Peter who got me the job moving water lines for his employer.

While we worked hard, we also got to spend some of our summer exploring and being kids together. Peter's father was quite strict with the kids but his mom, my aunt Zan, was the queen of all ladies. She championed to let us go enjoy some of the warm days outside of the fields. I remember once that summer we packed up the car and headed a few hours east to see Yellowstone park.

Back then, one could get their driver's license at the ripe old age of fourteen in Idaho. Peter was driving, I was riding in the passenger seat, and Peter's little brother, Ben, sat in the backseat. A large map engulfed my lap as I attempted to lead us through Yellowstone park. After Yellowstone, we took a trip north to Montana where we camped for the week. At one point, I lost our place on the map. Peter had me take over steering the car while he searched for our location among the fine print. Unused to driving from the passenger seat, we nearly ran into a ditch before Peter took back the wheel.

That summer, our boss lived just a few miles down a gravel road from my cousin's house. Due to the short distance, we typically rode motorcycles to get there. Parallel ruts snaked their way along the road making it look like a giant had dragged three fingers down the center. We drove our motorcycles in the ruts where passing cars had compacted the gravel. The loose gravel in between the ruts often caused the bikes to fishtail.

I was on my way to work to move the water lines at his house one morning. Although it was early, the air was already hot. I passed a potato field on the right on my way to his property. I could see a semicircle of darkened gravel a short distance ahead—evidence of sprinklers. Being hit in the face by spraying water while traveling at fifty-five miles per hour is no picnic. I swerved across the road and drove in the left rut to avoid the needling spray. I continued that way for a while without incident. Although it was the wrong side of the road to be driving on, I figured I would be able to see anyone coming my way. All the while, there was a gathering cloud of dust down the road that went unnoticed.

Before I knew it, a small two-seater car came whipping up over the hill in front of me. Whoever it was, they were flying. They likely assumed as I did that no one else would be on the road that early.

It is funny how a single moment can reveal all the mistakes made leading up to it. I remember thinking, *where's my helmet?* In less than a second, I had to make a decision that would likely determine the rest of my life, perhaps even end it. Multiple scenarios rushed through my mind. I could stay on course and collide with the car. Each of us was traveling over fifty miles per hour so, I would likely die instantly. *Or* I could veer to the left into the narrow pit beside the road and likely die. *Or* I could cut back to the right and possibly miss the collision, lose control of the bike and probably be seriously injured or die.

I could feel my heart pulsing uncontrollably. I let off the gas and squeezed my legs against the bike as tightly as I could. Jerking the handlebars and throwing my weight to the right to cut back to the other side of the road. Closing my eyes, I thought, *I'm dead. I'm dead. I'm dead.*

I heard a loud *tick.* When I opened my eyes a few seconds later I was surprised to be alive. I hadn't lost control of the bike or been completely annihilated by the car which seemed like the only two options just a second before. I got off the bike and walked up to the north side of my boss's house into the open bay doors of the garage.

My clothes seemed to be vibrating off my body. I knelt down and thanked God I hadn't died.

When I went to get back on the bike, my left foot missed the peg. When I looked down, I saw the peg had been bent back awkwardly at nearly a 45-degree angle. The realization of what had happened flooded into my body like ice water. The tick I had heard had been the car hitting the motorcycle peg. I had somehow tucked my legs in tight enough that I was unharmed. Even more miraculously, the impact did not knock me off the bike.

To fix the peg, I took the motorcycle to my uncle's shop. He removed the thick rubber and used a welding torch to heat the metal knob. My uncle then slipped a pipe over the knob to give himself leverage to bend it back. The peg had almost been ripped off the motorcycle. Yet, somehow, I walked away without a scratch.

. . .

Starting at a young age, I was immersed in sports. It was my dad's fault. In addition to teaching English at the high school, he also coached football and track. Coincidently, I played both sports until my biking accident in the ninth grade.

My dad was a dedicated coach. He was always doing something with his teams. He even drove the bus to take them to events. Because of this, his team members became frequent visitors in our home. I was a little boy then, rubbing shoulders with older guys I idolized. One athlete in particular became a permanent fixture in our family.

Danny Siemens was a basketball superstar from a broken home; his parents were divorced, and his dad liked the bottle. Danny frequently bailed his dad out of jail. He began spending more and more time at our house until it seemed like Danny was always there. He frequently went to church with us. I was a kid then, seven or so, but to me Danny was everything I wanted to be. He was well-liked, funny and an all-star basketball player. I once saw him make a half-court shot at the buzzer to win a game. That kind of thing made him hero material to me. He became so integrated into our family that when my eighth birthday came around, Danny was the person I asked to baptize me. I have always considered him a foster brother.

...

My mom's health was always poor. Yet, every year it seemed to get worse. Despite numerous exploratory surgeries, the doctors were at a loss. And yet, though she faced countless challenges of both body and mind, my lovely mother worked incredibly hard to maintain our home. It was no small task due to our family's growing size.

My parents had wanted more kids for years but with my mom's declining health, she couldn't carry another baby. When I was eight, they adopted a baby girl. My parents named her Richelle after Danny's older sister who died in a tragic accident when Danny was six. Two years later they adopted a baby boy. Zane made them young parents of five children in addition to the athletes who frequented our home.

Despite her physical struggles, my mom took pride in cleanliness and order; things were always spotless around the house. Some of my favorite memories with her involve her passion for gardening, especially flowers. She was always doing something in the gardens. As she got older and could no longer bend over to weed, she spent hours sitting in the dirt scooting from one area to another until everything was perfect.

. . .

Two years had passed since my biking accident and while I recovered fully—without any noticeable facial scars—I began to notice changes taking place in the right side of my chest and both of my arms. Despite my best efforts, I was losing muscle tone at an alarming rate.

My mom and I arrived at the neurology office in Yakima where *Dr. Roy Kokenge* (pronounced "cocaine") was emblazoned on a brass plaque outside the door. My mother's attempts at small talk during the car ride were met with silence and mumbled one-word responses. It was all I could manage due to the pit in my stomach. Dr. Kokenge was a specialist who graduated from the University of Washington in 1960. I pushed open the door and sat in the lobby as my mother talked with the receptionist.

Eventually, we were led back to a small room with two chairs and an examining table in the center. After more silent waiting, there was a small knock. Then a tall, slender man with black hair entered the room. He shook my hand and introduced himself as Dr. Kokenge while flashing me a well-intentioned smile.

After introductions were made, he instructed me to remove my shirt and jeans and lay down on the table. Wiping my damp hands across my jeans, I quickly undressed and climbed up onto the crinkling white paper. Dr. Kokenge then picked up a long needle with a colored end. He showed me the needles and explained what would happen next.

The lengthy needles were inserted into various muscles throughout my body. I tensed involuntarily as each needle sank deep beneath my skin into the muscles in my arms, legs, and chest. Dread built in my chest with each painful prick. I stared at a fixed point on the ceiling until it was over.

After he finished, Dr. Kokenge left the room to examine the results. My stomach was in knots as I redressed, and we waited. I couldn't face my mom. Instead, I continued to stare at the wall and willed myself to be well.

...

18

Growing up in such a sports-centered family, being physically active was a large part of who I was. Before we moved to Washington, we lived about fifteen miles southwest of Blackfoot, Idaho in a speck of a town called Pingree. Both of my parents grew up in southeast Idaho. My mom was from Grace, my dad from Roberts. They lived 120 miles apart, but both grew up involved in rodeos. Once upon a time, Mom had been a rodeo queen. My dad rode in rodeos throughout high school and into college. Naturally, he was asked to be a rodeo clown every year during the Celebration Day festivities on the 24th of July.

To me, Celebration Day was like a second 4th of July. Big metal bins full of beef were buried in the ground and made entire fields smell of smoky BBQ heaven. There were parades, games, fireworks, cook-outs and of course, the rodeo. Even kids could sign up for bronc riding. With my parents so involved, one of the first Celebration Days I can remember, I was determined to ride in the rodeo. I shared my plans with my dad. He tried to dissuade me saying, "Martin, it's not like riding the bucking calves at grandma's." But I wouldn't listen. Eventually, he gave in to my stubbornness and allowed me to sign up. A nervous excitement passed through me like a shot as I wrote my name on the paper.

My shirt clung to my back under the hot sun as I watched others try their hand at the animals. When my turn finally came, I mounted the young mustang bareback and was let out of the gate. A spirited horse, he took off. Within seconds I was bucked off. It all happened so fast. One second, I was on the horse, and the next, I was flipped over his head, and landed face first in the dirt. My dad jogged over to ask if I was alright. Other than a mouthful of dirt and bruised pride, I was fine. His face split into a characteristically wide smile as he helped me up. He resisted the urge to say I told you so. I wiped the muddy spittle from my face and smiled too. What an exhilarating thing it was to ride in a rodeo!

...

One of my proudest athletic moments was in fourth grade. Not only did I set a new school record of eighteen pull-ups that year, but I also nearly became an elementary school legend. My Physical Education teacher was a sprightly young guy who was a lot of fun. He and I sometimes bantered back and forth about who was faster. I was sure I would be able to stand my own against him. Finally, one day after school we met on the track to settle the debate once and for all.

Our entire class surrounded the starting line eager to witness the race. One student was in charge of timing the event. The smell of cut grass hung in the hot air. My heart was pounding as we lined up on the track. This was my moment.

At the signal, we both took off in a mad dash. I pumped my arms and ran as fast as my feet could carry me. Despite my shorter leg-span, we were neck and neck. At the last possible moment, my teacher pulled ahead of me. I crossed the line completely winded. I finished the fifty-yard dash in under seven seconds. Although I didn't win, I still felt like an elementary school legend; I was ten years old and I had *almost* beat my teacher.

. . .

After what seemed like an eternity, there was another quiet knock on the door followed by dark hair and a white coat. Dr. Kokenge wore a somber face this time. I knew what he was going to say, but I didn't want to hear it.

"Martin, I'm sorry to tell you that the results came back positive," Dr. Kokenge said. "They show you have muscular dystrophy."

Muscular dystrophy.

Those two words were rocks that shattered the fragile pane of hope left inside of me. If he said it, it must be true. I had suspected something wasn't right for some time, but I couldn't face it.

My mother had been recently diagnosed with muscular dystrophy herself. That must have been how she knew where to take me. It was a genetic disease, after all. Her own journey had been more laborious. For years, my mom went through one surgery after another trying to determine the cause of her declining health. Not only did those surgeries fail to provide answers, but they also placed a significant financial burden on our family.

Dr. Kokenge went on to explain that I had not one, but *two* types of muscular dystrophy: facioscapulohumeral and limb-girdle. At first, they were just strange words. But those words were already at war with my body. The battles for my arms and right shoulder had already begun, and my body was losing.

He explained, "When someone exercises, their muscles develop microscopic tears. A healthy body repairs the tears, and the muscle grows. However, muscular dystrophy impedes the repairing process which leaves the muscles unable to regenerate. It is a progressive disease which means it gets worse over time. Your mobility will be more limited as the muscles atrophy.

"Unfortunately, it often causes respiratory and heart problems that can result in death by early adulthood. Typically, I don't see progressive symptoms in someone as young as you are." He mentioned that the trauma of my previous accident had likely acted as a catalyst and triggered the disease to activate in my body.

A wave of fear washed over me and made it difficult to breathe. My mind flashed back to eight-year-old Martin sitting in class. Despite my reading disability, the teacher asked me to read in front of everyone. I stood and stumbled through; my tongue blundering awkwardly over the letters. The kids snickered. I finished, then darted back into my seat looking at the ground. My mouth tasted of copper.

From that point on, whenever he asked for a volunteer to read, I always avoided eye contact. But it didn't stop the kids from teasing me. Inevitably, they mocked, "Oh, Martin will read it! Martin will read it!" It seemed that they laughed uncontrollably whenever the teacher asked me to read. I never understood why he couldn't just read things himself.

I sat in Doctor Kokenge's office and despaired. I knew the teasing was going to start again. Yet, this time it would be worse. Hiding a reading disability was fairly simple. However, muscular dystrophy was something people would be able to see at school, at church, in the grocery store. I was going to be different and it was going to be on display for the world to mock. I was seventeen and this doctor had just pronounced my death sentence.

. . .

When I was younger, I sometimes got really angry. It was a trait I must have inherited from my mom because my dad was a cool customer—always in control. Something I appreciated about him is that whenever we were disciplined as kids, he never hit us in a fit of anger. He sat us down, looked us in the eye and said, "This is going to hurt me more than it hurts you." I learned to believe him. It hurt him to spank us, but he did it because that was the way things were done back then. Despite his example of self-control, the anger inside me frequently came out in fits of rage.

In ninth grade, the stocky school bully caught me in an alleyway and tried to take my lunch money. I refused to give it up. After attempts to badger the money out of me, he became annoyed with my resistance and began to bang my head against the side of a brick wall. He beat me up badly that day. Even though I kept my money, I was furious about the encounter. I didn't seek revenge on him, but once I got home, I went to my room, shut the door and threw things around—totally out of control.

This time, it was not my lunch money someone tried to take; this disease was going to take my life. When we got home from the doctor's office, I went to my room and shut the door. Then, I gave in to the allurement of anger. It felt nice to lose control. I turned up my radio and let the music blare while the rage consumed me.

Show Me Mercy

For as long as I could remember my dad dreamed of owning a farm of his own one day. This dream became a reality when I was in high school. After nearly two decades of teaching ninth grade English, coaching both football and track, and consulting for other farms, he had finally saved enough money to buy an orchard outside of Zillah, Washington. It took everything we had to buy that place.

The property was an established cherry and pear orchard. There were thirteen-acres of cherries and nearly forty-acres of pears. The house, a rambler, sat back from the road on a hill overlooking the valley. Like all our other houses growing up, it was simple. Kirk and Kaelin had both moved out which left me, Richelle and Zane at home with my mom and dad.

Over the years we lived there, my parents made it their own. My dad built a major addition onto the home, a two-story master suite. The bottom floor had a sunken living room area while upstairs housed the master bedroom and bathroom. Part of making the house their own included adding aspects of their personalities.

My dad's love of rocks inspired a large lava rock fireplace surround. A real statement piece, it was nearly eight feet wide and stacked all the way to the ceiling. For her part, my mom spent long hours cultivating the gardens, so we were always surrounded by beautiful flowers. They invested so much of who they were into that home, and it was in that house that we nearly lost everything.

On a Friday evening in late spring, after months of work, our first year's crop started to bloom. I came home from a date and fell asleep in my room. Around 1:00 a.m. my dad rushed in. His hand still gripped the doorknob as he roused me from sleep. He desperately needed my help in the orchards. I quickly threw on clothes and ran outside. The chilly night air instantly cleared my foggy mind.

For a farmer, spring is a precarious time. Once the fruit trees begin to blossom, the small buds growing inside the flowers are extremely susceptible to the cold. If not kept warm enough, they die from exposure. This killing temperature is known as critical temperature and the delicate buds can only withstand it for up to thirty minutes before freezing to death. In the hours following their demise, they blacken inside. Farmers can lose an entire crop in one frosty night.

One way to prevent frost damage is by smudging. A smudge pot is a large metal stove of sorts. The wide circular base is filled with gallons of oil for burning. Out of the center climbs a skinny metal neck filled with holes. The top of the neck is covered with a removable cap. A smudge pot's work to combat frost is twofold. First, the burning oil produces some heat. But, more importantly, smudge pots produce large amounts of smoke that blanket the orchard and protect the buds from exposure.

The rows of cherry trees ran perpendicular to the small valley in our orchard. We kept smudge pots staggered between trees throughout the orchard for moments like this. As the early hours marched on, the frost began to creep up from the valley and into the rising trees on either side. My dad ran frantically between the lines of trees lighting and opening the smudge pot caps, but the frost was faster. He needed more help, or the crop would be lost.

I saw Zane trying to help but he was too little to do much. Mom was back at the house. Her health left her nearly bedridden. She had to rely on Dad and me to save the orchard. I set my jaw and got to work as rapidly as I could. My dad lit one side of the orchard's smudge pots and I lit the other.

Though effective, smudge pots could be tricky to control. With a limited amount of oil, we had to manage the burn rate, so they didn't run out of fuel too quickly. Just before dawn is always the darkest and coldest part of the night. We had to time the burn to last until the sun came up. Otherwise, we would lose the fruit.

We sprinted like madmen between the trees. Branches tore at our clothes and skin as we raced to keep the frost from the trees and their tender cargo. Because we had risked everything for this farm, we could not afford to lose the fruit, especially not this first season. It would ruin us.

Just before dawn, Dad and I had all the smudge pots' lids off. Flames shot up over a foot and a half from the tops of those little chimneys between the trees. If anyone had passed by unaware, they might have thought we were trying to set fire to the orchard. Finally, after what seemed like an eternity, the sun broke over the horizon.

With the rising of the sun, I fell to the ground panting. I was relieved the long night had ended, but our trial was not over. We had yet to see if our efforts had been enough to save the orchard. Richelle and Zane joined me exhausted on the ground. Together we watched my father carefully walk the rows picking random buds from the branches with a pocketknife. I can still see his hands shaking as he cut them vertically, one by one, to survey the damage of the night.

The first bud was blackened inside. As was the second. To our despair, nearly all the buds he sampled had withered. The precious baby buds had succumbed to the frost. As we sat in the dirt, I watched my stoic father weep, "I've lost everything."

Despair slammed into my chest. My dad had worked his entire life for this, it wasn't fair. We had done all we could, and it wasn't enough. Instead of sliding into despair himself, my father asked us to kneel. We each dragged our weary bodies from our reclined positions and onto our knees on the dewy ground.

My father bowed his head and pleaded, "Lord--" His voice cracked over the word. "I've been faithful," he paused. "I've paid my tithing. I've done the right things; I need a blessing here…"

The Lord heard my father's heartfelt prayer. Although all seemed lost, that season God breathed life back into those trees. A few months later the orchard pulled out of it. In twenty-years, that season was the largest yield of cherries the orchard had ever seen.

…

With my diagnosis I knew I would eventually have to give up sports, but I wasn't ready to let go quite yet. So, junior year I signed up for tennis. As the spring progressed, I noticed my right arm was getting weaker. Despite our workouts, my muscles were shrinking. I wrote it off again and again. I attempted to smother the sinking feeling in my stomach until I couldn't feel it anymore. I knew things would get worse, but I didn't expect it to happen so quickly.

I quickly reached the point where I couldn't continue. My chest was too weak to produce any power in my swing. More than that however, tennis required large amounts of sprinting. Without muscle strength in my arms, running became impossible. By the end of the season, I couldn't lift any weight with my right arm. It was a real mental blow the next year when I had to have my P.E. credit waived. Even worse, my fears were realized when some kids at school began to call me "weeny arm".

While they laughed at my expense, what those kids could not see were the harsh realities of this disease. I couldn't even lift my arms above my head anymore. It made everyday tasks seem unconquerable. I learned to use what little strength I had—coupled with whatever I could leverage around me—to figure out new ways around obstacles. For instance, determined to wash my own hair, I used my left arm to prop my right elbow up against the wall in the shower so I could reach the top of my head.

It was during this time I felt most alone. How does one grieve the loss of something as intangible as the future? I found myself folding inward. I withdrew from friends and family because I was so angry all the time with how unfair life turned out to be. I was only halfway through high school; my life was just beginning. I had been making plans for a future of working on the farm with my dad, of getting married and playing with my kids someday. None of that was possible now. Who would marry me? Besides, I couldn't be a burden like that on someone. And kids? They were out of the picture as far as I was concerned—this was a genetic disease after all.

I was lucky that not everyone left me to be alone. I was dating a girl at the time, Linda, who helped me through it all. She brought little rays of light into my ever-darkening world. She gave me hope that when one dream dies, there are new ones we can find if we are willing to look.

. . .

By the time senior year rolled around I began to take on more responsibility at home. My dad took on more orchard consulting jobs throughout the valley to help cover my mom's pile of medical bills. This left me to run much of the farm while he was away. It didn't conflict with school because I had enough credits to drop down to part-time and still graduate with my class.

While I could no longer run, I could still walk. Daily life included waking up before dawn, changing the water lines, then getting ready for school. I attended my classes, then headed home for lunch. After a quick bite, I was back outside spraying, picking, pruning, or mowing. On Saturdays and school holidays, I was up at four and out in the fields until after dark. I spent time hiring and running the crews that helped during the busy picking months from summer into fall.

As I continued to lose strength, I had to invent new ways to accomplish familiar tasks. For example, it used to be a simple thing to move the water lines. Then I lost the ability to pull them off the ground with my bicep strength alone. Through trial and error, I discovered that if I kept my arms locked at the elbows and bent over to grab a pipe, I could use my lower back and leg muscles to maneuver the pipes around the fields. To get onto a tractor, I used my left leg to step onto the first stair and then brought my right leg up to meet it. When I was close enough, I grabbed the steering wheel to keep from falling and used the wheel to flip myself into the seat.

...

When I was eighteen, I wanted to get my own pickup. My parents helped my two older siblings buy their first cars. I approached my dad about buying a pickup and was somewhat surprised when he responded, "Okay, but you're going to have to earn it." What I didn't realize was that by the time I was old enough to drive, finances were too tight for my parents to help. I had to find another way to get a truck.

I ended up finding pruning work that winter for a guy who owned a thirteen-acre orchard nearby. My dad dropped me off in the frosty mornings. I quickly got to work to keep from freezing. There were just over a thousand trees to attend to, which kept me busy all winter. Each tree required personal attention. I began each morning lugging around a three-legged orchard ladder to the base of a new tree. Then, with a pruning saw that always reminded me of the grim reaper's scythe, I removed all the branches around two inches in diameter. Climbing up the ladder I then used lopping shears on the smaller branches. Finally, I had hand pruning shears for the small twigs. I worked slowly but methodically and found ways to get around problems that came up due to my limited mobility. Repeating this process tree after tree kept me warm throughout the snowy winter.

After months of intense labor, I had saved enough money to buy my own pickup. She was a 1954 six-cylinder Chevy pickup. The car was older than I was with an engine that needed replacing. Thankfully, my dad knew a guy who helped us rebuild it. While she did not win any beauty contests—the flaking orange paint being nearly two-toned from the sun—she was beautiful because she was mine.

...

After graduation, it was time for me to keep the promise I made to God after my biking accident. So, I prepared myself for missionary service. My parents were struggling financially, and I knew it would be even more difficult without my help on the farm. I also knew the Lord had spared my life and my time had come to serve a mission. I received my assignment to the Colorado, Denver mission and reported for service on July 20, 1976.

My parents drove Kirk, Richelle, Zane and me to Salt Lake City, Utah. I sat in the car in my suit as a freshly set-apart missionary. Everything felt surreal—like it wasn't actually me this was all happening to.

We spent the night at a hotel in Salt Lake. The next morning, we all knelt together around the hotel bed for a family prayer. Although three years older than I, Kirk had not yet served a mission. In fact, he had wandered from the teachings of Christ altogether. When it was time for me to go, Kirk turned to me and said, "Now you're the oldest in the family. I know I need to straighten my life out." An egg-sized lump formed in my throat. We hugged and I said goodbye to my siblings who stayed at the hotel while my parents dropped me off at the Missionary Training Center.

I walked through the doors carrying my suitcase. I could scarcely believe I was finally there. At the same time, things were beginning to sink in. This would be a new start for me. I was leaving behind all the people who bullied me as a kid. This new setting would also distance me from the disappointment of not being able to play sports anymore. I looked at it as an opportunity to overcome everything that burdened me and held me back.

The idea that no one knew me was electrifying. I could become whoever I wanted to be. There was no former self to box me in. I set a personal goal to focus on improving my reading through diligent study. I did not want my reading disability to hold me back anymore. I was going to take this fresh start and make it worthwhile. With that in mind, I vowed I was going to be the best missionary the Lord had ever seen.

I arrived in Boulder, Colorado at the beginning of August. My trainer was a fellow Washingtonian named Elder Walker. We got along right away. Our area served the Colorado University singles congregation. It was intimidating for me because they really put the fear of God into new missionaries about avoiding girls.

During my first week, we got a call one evening from a girl in the congregation who asked to speak with me. She introduced herself and told me she had seen me at church on Sunday. She wanted to let me know how cute I was. I dropped the phone back on the receiver as if it were on fire. My face flushed, I turned to my companion in horror. He and another set of missionaries visiting the apartment were howling with laughter. It had all been a prank they concocted to haze the new missionary.

. . .

I had been in Boulder a short time when a young man began attending the singles congregation. He was a dynamic guy who loved sharing the good news of the gospel. He had recently returned from his own missionary service in England. At the time, there were seven main lessons missionaries were supposed to teach anyone interesting in joining the Church of Jesus Christ.

This young man contacted our mission president and asked to demonstrate something from his mission. During a missionary conference, this former Elder took the stage with President Lambourne and his assistants. In front of numerous church members as well as the missionaries in that area, he taught a lesson about recognizing the Spirit. He used verses from the Bible to teach what the Spirit feels like. He helped those on stage to understand that what they were feeling as they spoke together was the Spirit of the Lord.

President Lambourne was so impressed by this lesson that he asked the young man to work with his assistants to write it up in the teaching format used at the time. He wanted to adapt it to the people living in the Colorado mission and implement it throughout the missionaries' teaching.

...

Before I knew it, I had already been on my mission for ten months. The days could be burdensome, but I had never felt so purposeful. I had recently been transferred from Colorado to Dodge City, Kansas. My companion and I walked and biked because we didn't have a car. I enjoyed being outside. It also made it easier to meet new people.

After a few weeks of the increased physical activity, I noticed alarming changes in my body. My right thigh seemed to be dissolving. Fear began to creep back into my heart. I recognized what was happening, but I tried to ignore it.

Certainly, God would not do that to me. Not now, not here. Yet, deep inside I knew the truth. It caused something inside of me to snap. *Here I am serving the Lord. I am doing everything He has asked me to do. I am being obedient. Why is this happening to me?* A tidal wave of emotion threatened to drown me. Rather than the burning anger I was used to experiencing, this time I felt hurt. *How could You do this to me?*

Over the next few weeks, I spent my personal time in prayer and reflection. I tried to come to terms with how God could allow this to happen. I knelt at the edge of my bed in prayer one evening—my forehead resting on my folded arms as I pleaded for help—tears streamed down my face as I called out for God to show me some mercy.

Eventually, the Spirit brought peace to the turmoil in my heart. The idea pressed upon my mind to ask my mission president for a priesthood blessing. Two months later, the opportunity presented itself to make the request.

In July of 1977, we learned our mission was going to be split. My area was to become part of the Missouri,

Independence mission. During my last interview with President Lambourne, he told me he was sad to see one of his best missionaries go. Although he was a man of average build, he had a bearing that made him seem taller. Other than my father, he was the man I loved and respected most in the world.

A few minutes into the interview, I steeled myself.

"President?" I said, my face full of concern.

"Yes, Elder Van Leuven?"

"I wanted to let you know that my right leg has been giving me trouble."

I looked at the ground and tried to keep my voice even. "It is beginning to atrophy like my arms did before I came out on my mission." After a short pause I continued, "I've been praying about it and I was instructed by the Spirit to ask you for a blessing." My blue eyes flitted up and stared earnestly into his. "Through the power of the priesthood, I know you can heal me."

JoAnne

After completing my missionary service, I returned to work with my dad in the orchard. I could think of nothing better for my life than to spend it farming with my father.

I jumped on our green John Deere tractor one morning and drove out to the cherry fields. The tractor was comfortable enough, with armrests and a cushioned back to support hours of mowing. I cruised into the orchard and slipped the Power Take-Off into gear. Once engaged, the PTO shaft spun rapidly behind me powering the swing-arm mower that extended behind the tractor and to the right.

It was important to keep the grass manageable to deter mice and diseases among the trees, so we mowed about once a month. I mowed along in the hot sun and filled the air with the scent of freshly cut grass. After a long morning, I was finally approaching the farthest reaches of the orchard. Because the trees were over twenty years old, many had branches that jutted out into the narrow paths. As I approached such a branch, I leaned to the left to avoid it while attempting to mow close to the trunk. Unfortunately, I was too close.

Before I could react, I was pinned against the back of the seat by a sturdy branch. The mower simultaneously plowed into the trunk of the tree. The tires began to spit up dirt as they struggled against the trunk. There was an enormous amount of pressure on my torso. Then, I heard a loud *crack* emanate from my chest as I was flipped backward over the seat. I instinctively clutched my feet around the steering wheel to keep myself from plummeting—to my death or serious dismemberment—into the spinning PTO shaft. Thankfully, the mower was still caught against the tree which gave me time to wrestle myself back into the seat.

I couldn't breathe. Once in the seat, I shifted the tractor out of gear and fell to the ground. The freshly cut grass stained my pants at the knees. I laid for a minute and tried to catch my breath, but it was impossible. I could only manage half-breaths. Alone and far from help, I realized I was not out of danger yet. With difficulty, I forced myself back onto the tractor and shifted it into gear. It didn't move. I looked back to my right and saw the mowing arm still stuck against the tree. I backed the tractor up to get momentum. Then, I popped the clutch into first gear which jolted me forward and slammed the mower against the tree. With a loud metal screech, the mower broke free. I drove back to the house over two miles away. Struggling for breath, I drove the tractor over the lawn to the back door. My mother saw me from the kitchen window and rushed outside wearing the apron I made her in my ninth-grade home economics class.

"Martin?"

I fell from the tractor to the ground.

She ran to me. "Martin!"

Unable to catch my breath, I whispered, "Go get the car."

My mom brought the car around and rushed me to the emergency room in Yakima.

The doctor inspected me and ordered x-rays. I had a broken rib which punctured the outer layer before my lung. He said it was a miracle I wasn't severed in half. That experience was a testimony to me of the protective power of temple covenants.

...

When I returned from my missionary service, I gave a report to a high council regarding my experiences. After that report, I received various invitations to speak at church services throughout the area. One such assignment was to the congregation in Ellensburg which served young single adults attending Central Washington University and the surrounding area.

The congregation held Sunday services in an old institute building. It was a recreational room filled with rows of folding chairs and a center aisle. When I stood to speak, my eye caught on a beautiful, brown haired girl in the back row. All these years later, I still remember her blue and white plaid shirt under a jean vest paired with a denim skirt. While I didn't believe in soulmates, I had the impression she'd be a good wife for me.

I went to introduce myself after the service. Meeting her that day changed my life. I learned she was attending Central, so I decided to take a break from farming with my father and go to college. Armed with her name and a good first impression, my grand plan was to show up at Central and sweep JoAnne Lee off her feet. I found an off-campus apartment and signed up for a few classes including Middle Eastern Religions. Most importantly, I began to attend church there, intent on asking her out.

. . .

January 8th, 1979 was a Monday. During a church activity that night I finally tracked down my mystery girl. We talked throughout the evening and I told her I was driving south to Yakima to see my dad in the hospital the next day. I wanted to see her again, so I invited her to come with me. Her acceptance turned my invitation into our first date.

During the forty-minute drive we continued to get to know each other. There was something special about her that set me at ease and made me feel safe. It felt like I had known her for years. There was also an undeniable spark between us. Pretty soon we were holding hands; her touch sent sparks like lightning up my arm. I wanted to make sure she was feeling the same way I was, so I asked if she had ever done that so quickly with a guy before. She continued to trace her thumb along mine and shook her head. My heart soared and I knew our connection was mutual.

We entered the hospital and were assaulted by the smell of disinfectant. That smell had a tendency to make me slightly nauseous. We navigated our way to my dad's room. He was pretty drugged when we walked in. When he saw JoAnne he said, "Oh! Is this the one you're marrying?"

Dad! What are you doing?

Mortified on the inside, I tried to play it cool. "Ah, she's pretty. I don't know…" The higher register of my voice betrayed my embarrassment. I turned to JoAnne and whispered I had never said that to my dad before.

There was an awkward pause and then I remembered.

"Dad, this is JoAnne. JoAnne, this is my dad."

The next week JoAnne invited me to her apartment for dinner. I remember thinking: *this woman knows how to cook!* A few days later I invited her to my place for dinner. I made steak.

A few weeks after we started dating JoAnne turned nineteen. Everything felt so natural between us. I was completely smitten. I was also motivated to make our relationship permanent before she could change her mind. In those brief three weeks of dating, we were already discussing a future together. Things continued to progress and in February, I found myself at Zales picking out a ring.

The day finally came for me to propose to JoAnne. We had talked about marriage and knew it was what we both wanted, but I was still nervous to ask. I invited her to my apartment. After we talked for a while, I asked her to reach into my front pocket. Inside was a small box. I opened it to reveal a gold ring. The center diamond had a cluster of three smaller diamonds swirled underneath it. Holding out the ring, I asked JoAnne to marry me.

Before she could answer, there was a knock at the door. Reflexively, I moved to answer it. It was a man proselyting for another church. It was like a switch flipped in my mind and I went from romantic Martin to missionary Martin. We began to discuss our beliefs and the conversation must have gone on for a while because when he left, I realized JoAnne had gone as well— without answering me! While I assumed her decision to take the ring was an affirmative response, I still tried to find her. I later found out she had gone to tell her friends the exciting news of our engagement.

It seems silly all these years later that our wedding date was set because of a bet. My last missionary companion and I agreed before returning home that if either of us married within the year, we owed the other a plane ticket to the wedding. Since he was from Hawaii, it would have been a considerable sum to tack on to our wedding budget. To avoid the expense and stay true to my word, we prolonged our engagement and set the date a year to the day of my return. This date also coincided with my departure for missionary service and made it quite meaningful to me.

We were married on the 20th of July. JoAnne wore a white dress with long lacy sleeves and a short, round train. Her brown hair was curled perfectly under a white sun hat. She was absolutely radiant. I wore a dark suit with my hair parted in the middle and gelled into place. Though I was nearly three years her senior, my lanky features left me looking more like a young teenager.

Construction on the Seattle temple—which we have since attended most of our lives—would not be completed until the next year. But being young and in love like we were, it didn't matter which temple we were married in. We chose the Logan, Utah temple. It was there that we were sealed together for time and all eternity. Marrying her there that day was the best decision of my life.

Making Ends Meet

After we were married, I took over my dad's role on the farm. Despite the semester at school my body seemed to remember the routine. To be honest, it felt good to be back outside after months in a classroom. It didn't take long to feel like I had never left.

JoAnne and I lived in a small one-bedroom apartment in town. She taught at a local school there. Things started off well enough, but a few months into our marriage my dad began to hint that life could not continue as we had planned. My mom's medical bills had stockpiled over the last few years. Unable to keep up, they were going to lose the farm.

Sometimes I wonder if my mother ever grieved for the life she could have had. I know she was grateful to have my dad and us kids, but in the prime of her life both her mind and body began to manifest their genetic irregularities which made living a normal life impossible. Life was not kind to her. Before she was fifty, muscular dystrophy ravaged my mother's hips and confined her to a bed for the rest of her life. It was also discovered that she suffered from a rare hormone disorder known as Addison's. Finally, she fought breast cancer before she died at the age of seventy-three. Despite it all, I knew she did all she could for our family and that she loved me in her own way.

The future I had envisioned for so long was no longer an option. My dad was devastated things were turning out this way. My heart ached not only for myself, but for him. He was losing his dream. The farm he had worked so hard for would be lost. He graciously began to seek alternatives for my livelihood. The answer, he thought, seemed to be in the restaurant business. This conclusion was drawn from the success of a cousin who had become quite wealthy running, and eventually selling, a restaurant. He used the profits to start a financial consulting business in Sunnyside. Using his cousin's path as a model, my dad reached out to a friend who owned a local restaurant.

I came in salt-stained from the field one evening to find my dad sitting at the dining room table with a dark blond man whom I presumed to be Dean Stokes. Together, we discussed the possibility of me working at Stokes Burger Ranch. I didn't have a desire to work in the restaurant business, especially not for someone with Dean's reputation—being intense and even aggressive toward employees. But with a new bride, I had bigger things to consider than what I wanted.

The plan was to learn the restaurant business from Dean at his Sunnyside restaurant and eventually buy a second restaurant together. Under his mentorship, I would run the new place and we would split the profits. The offer was enticing enough; I mean, what other choice did I have?

It did not take long for Dean to live up to his reputation. He was a forceful guy, always pushing people to work harder. When JoAnne was hired, Dean berated her and the other employees and left JoAnne in tears. It was the only time Dean and I ever had a problem. JoAnne resigned within the week.

I could not afford to leave, however, so I continued showing up in hopes that a better future would manifest itself. I once covered a three-hundred-dollar lunch hour all by myself. Back in the kitchen, I pulled $1.50 hamburgers off the grill six at a time, nearly tripping over myself while trying to keep up with the orders.

Before I knew it, months rolled into years and the elusive second restaurant seemed forever out of reach.

I worked grueling seventy-hour weeks at Stokes Burger Ranch and only brought home $600 a month. My body was worn down and I did not know how long I could continue. I couldn't quit. We had a future to consider, and that future included a growing family.

JoAnne became pregnant about eight months after we were married. We were ecstatic about the pregnancy and more determined than ever to put our noses to the grind to provide for our child. Thus, ensued a string of part-time and odd jobs to supplement our income. Some of these odd jobs were one-time events brought about through happenstance.

For example, we had a friend who worked on a chicken farm. One night he needed help gathering chickens to be sent for processing. JoAnne and I, with a few other friends, spent an entire evening wrangling chickens. We arrived at the farm and entered large chicken sheds. We were immediately overwhelmed by the stench. As we looked down, we easily found the culprit; we were inches deep in chicken waste. The sheds were illuminated by colored lights that served to blind the chickens to make it easier to capture them. We were shown how to bend and grab the chickens and thread their legs between our fingers. By doing this, we were able to hold three flailing, upside-down chickens in one hand and two in the other. Outside, we loaded them into crates of ten that were then stacked onto a pallet. Once the pallets were full, a forklift loaded them into a semi-truck. Back and forth we went, collecting chickens. After hours of chicken poop, flying feathers and hysterical clucking, we were finally finished. We left that night with ruined shoes, gouges on our arms, and about $60 in our pockets for the trouble. It was back-breaking, dirty work and it made me grateful to have a stable job at the restaurant, even with its downfalls.

We also had multiple part-time jobs to help pay the bills. Such was the case with my experience serving legal papers as a process server. I was hired by a small company. When I started, there was only one other person serving papers. Despite our small number, we handled a large volume of documents; from people being sued, to divorce, and subpoenas ordering people to court, we did it all. There were a few unsavory characters I met along the way.

One of my first weeks on the job, my manager called me to his desk where he handed me paperwork for a man named Roy Ross. He also gave me specific instructions regarding this serve. He explained that Roy was recently released from the State Penitentiary for firing a gun in Toppenish town square. Ironically, he lost a big toe during the incident because his gun, a .45, misfired as he drew it.

My manager continued, "I want you to make sure to catch him in a public place where there are a lot of people around. He shouldn't be packing, but he probably will be. So, I want you to take the police with you when you serve this guy." He must have sensed my apprehension because he added, "Just go to the police department and get someone to go with you."

I knew his warning was well-founded. In the month I had worked there, my coworker had been sent to the hospital with a broken pelvis after a guy came at her with a baseball bat.

I went inside the Police Station and stood in front of a large officer who looked up at me expectantly from his desk.

"Hi, I'm Martin Van Leuven."

"Hello Martin, what can we do for you?" he asked, looking back down through some paperwork.

"Well, I'm a process server and I'm supposed to go deliver a subpoena to someone who just got out of prison and is likely armed. I was told by my office to come here and have an officer go with me."

The officer looked up and chuckled. He called out to a colleague a few feet away in conversation with another officer. "Hey! You've got to hear this. This guy wants us to go with him to deliver a subpoena because the guy just got out of the pen."

He and the other officers laughed.

The large officer at the desk swiveled his attention back to me, "I'm sorry man, that's not our problem. But I wish you luck." He went back to his paperwork.

Another officer walked over as I began to leave and asked who I was serving. "Roy Ross," I said, showing him the paperwork. He told me that Roy typically hung out at the Branding Iron in Toppenish. I thanked him for the tip and left.

In my short time on the job, I had already developed habits to help me serve papers more effectively. It was required to get the person to admit who they were before I could serve them the paperwork. Once they confirmed their identity, I could drop the papers and go—even if they wouldn't accept them. I wanted my hands free to avoid seeming suspicious and to allow me greater flexibility (in case I needed to defend myself or get out of there quickly). To accomplish this, I sealed the paperwork inside an envelope. Using an envelope gave me time to leave before the person realized what I had given them. Most importantly in this case, it gave Roy less time to shoot the messenger.

The Branding Iron Restaurant and Lounge was a single-story red building. I was slightly encouraged to find it more of a small-town diner than a pub. I tucked Roy's envelope into the back of my pants, leaving only an inch sticking out against my tucked-in shirt, and went inside. I found the hostess. "Do you happen to know a guy by the name of Roy Ross?"

She nodded. "Yeah. He's over there." She pointed across the restaurant. "In the corner sitting with those other people."

My eyes followed her finger. It was a typical diner set-up with a bar, tabletops, and bright plastic leather seats. In the corner booth sat a group of people chatting over burgers and fries.

The pressure in my chest released a little. More people meant more witnesses. I decided to take a nonchalant approach. If I used my baby face to appear like a young kid, perhaps I could get him to admit his identity without a confrontation. I approached the corner booth. When everyone turned to look at me, I said, "Hey, I was over there talking, and they said you're Roy Ross..."

A weathered man with a deep voice from the middle of the group said, "Yeah, whadabout it?"

Well, that was easy. I reached back and pulled the envelope out from my waistline and held it out to him. Instead of taking the envelope as I had hoped, he said, "I want you to open that up and hold it open so I can read it."

My palms dampened. I fumbled for words. "Um...my bosses told me I'm not supposed to do that." He continued to insist. His volume increased after each refusal.

After a few choruses, a woman at his table chimed in. "Ah, come on Roy. Don't give the young man a hard time." Roy continued to badger me for another twenty minutes to open the envelope and disclose the contents. I continued to stand my ground. After more interjections from his tablemates, he finally took the envelope. I turned and exited the restaurant before he changed his mind.

Traumatic situations bind people together. As newlyweds, JoAnne served papers with me sometimes. One morning I had papers for a man out in White Swan on the Yakama Indian Reservation. An extremely rough area, we anticipated trouble. We pulled up to the house and I saw a man working in a shop nearby. I grabbed the paperwork and left JoAnne in the passenger seat. I approached the shop and saw the man was young and thin, dressed in greasy clothes. With one glance I knew he could beat me up. He turned toward the sound of my footsteps.

I asked for him by name.

"Yeah," he replied. "Who are you?" he said, squinting out into the sun.

"I have this for you," I said. I held the paperwork out to him.

He tensed. His eyes flicked to the right and he reached for a pipe wrench laying on the work bench. "No. You're not going to leave that here," he said. He pointed at me with the wrench for emphasis.

"Well, I'm supposed to."

"You get in your car," he said, gesturing with the wrench, "and get off my property. Now."

I may be brave, but I'm not stupid. I returned to my car and turned over the ignition. I could see him watching me closely through the window. I opened my door and dropped the paperwork on the ground. Before I could shift the car into gear, he had covered the distance between us, grabbed the paperwork and ripped open my car door.

JoAnne screamed, "This guy's going to kill you!"

I held my left arm over my face as the wrench came barreling toward me. My arm absorbed his blow as he threw the paperwork into the car. The papers landed on JoAnne's lap in the passenger seat. I reached for them. He held up the pipe wrench and threatened, "I'll take your window out. Don't you even think about it."

I closed the door and let the clutch out to jolt us into a forward roll. When he was even with the back bumper, I cracked my door and threw the paperwork on the ground once more. I called out, "You've been served, sucker!" before high tailing it out of there. JoAnne and I laughed about the near-death experience as we sped away. Adrenaline rushed through our veins as a deep purple bruise flowered across my arm.

I accepted another part-time position collecting on bad checks written to a local grocery store. Whenever a check bounced, I tracked down the person and physically collected the money for their purchase that hadn't cleared. This job morphed into security work for the store as well.

Before cameras, employees watched customers for suspicious behavior. When I worked security, there was a back room with a ladder that led to wooden scaffolding in the ceiling. My job was to sit and observe people throughout the store. There were mirrors hung around to catch different angles. They made it easier for me to catch people who tried to shoplift. Whenever someone stole, I called the police to deal with the thief.

One day I noticed a large woman in a red coat eating grapes in the produce section. Now, I had occasionally seen people eat a grape or two as they shopped, but this lady was really going for it! She stood there eating grapes by the handful. What was I to do? I had never seen anyone audacious enough to blatantly eat so much produce. It was obvious she hadn't paid for it, but she was consuming the evidence. It was genius.

I located the store owner and alerted him of the situation. I said, "Hey, I don't know what to do. This lady is eating grapes over in produce. She is just packing them down. She's a large lady..." gesturing with my hands, I continued, "I mean, she's *really* big..."

He looked at me and said, "Is she wearing a red coat?"

"Yes!" I exclaimed. He must have seen her as well.

He suppressed a smile. "Don't worry about it. That's my wife."

My eyes widened. I removed my foot from my mouth and mumbled an apology before returning to my post.

...

It was discouraging to spend most of our hard-earned money on rent. Yet, like most people our age, we couldn't see how we would ever be able to buy a house. Even with all our jobs, we were living paycheck to paycheck. At this rate, we would never have enough for a down payment. If, by some miracle we did find the money, interest rates in those days were in the double digits. It seemed impossible—until it happened.

A little over a year after we were married, we scrounged together the money from Stokes and our other jobs. With it, we were able to squeeze our way into a fourteen by fifty-two-foot mobile home in Yakima for $11,000. Three months before JoAnne was due with our first child, the trailer gave us more space for our growing family. We were able to get a loan for the trailer, but the 20% interest rate left us barely able to cover our mortgage. We reviewed our finances for the coming months— factoring in newborn expenses—and decided to move the mobile home to Granger, about twenty miles southeast of Yakima. We didn't know anyone there, but we discovered a mobile home park that offered a cheaper rate than what we currently paid. It seemed like the logical choice. It wasn't until we were there that we realized the mistake we made.

The park in Granger was designed around a circular street with mobile homes on either side. Our lot was located near the entrance in the inner circle. It didn't take long to realize our neighbors to the north sold drugs out of their house. There were nights when several cars waited in a line behind our house (like a fast food drive-through).

Our time in Granger wasn't all bad. In December, shortly after moving in, JoAnne and I decided to make and sell Christmas wreaths. I cut down a tree for material and JoAnne fashioned the wreaths together. We went door to door selling wreaths in the frosty air. Just after Christmas, after nine months of anxious waiting, our son Myles joined our family. The holiday season was aglow with extra magic that year. A few months later, we started a janitorial service. For the most part, we cleaned local businesses at night. We washed windows at the motorcycle shop and refinished the floor at Dairy Queen while Myles slept beside us in the car seat. We were determined to carve out a place for ourselves in the world. Other things became less important—even sleep. On the night of my twenty-sixth birthday, after working all day at Stokes, JoAnne and I cleaned for eight hours. It was grueling work, but we were doing what had to be done.

We kept our eyes open and when a spot became available at a trailer park in Sunnyside the next year, we leaped at the chance to move. We left Granger and never looked back.

...

A year later, I left Stokes Burger Ranch and began working at DB's restaurant two days later. I made about $200 more per month, but the hours were exhausting. DB's was a full-service restaurant which meant I typically worked seventy to ninety hours a week. My shift started at two p.m. and ended at one or two a.m. This new schedule left me no time to work our other jobs including the janitorial business. I worked as hard as I could and over the next three years, I only took one week off.

Once we gave up the janitorial business, JoAnne started watching kids during the week. By watching eight kids along with Myles she was able to double our income. The next few years passed by in a blur. Every day was the same. JoAnne got up in the morning with Myles. She changed him, made breakfast, got herself and Myles dressed and ready for the day before kids began to show up at the house. In the later morning, I got up, showered, and had lunch with them before leaving for work. JoAnne cooked, cleaned, and watched kids all day—while trying to keep them relatively quiet so I could get some sleep.

Once or twice a week, I took jobs process serving before my shift at DB's. After work, I came home in the middle of the night to a clean house and JoAnne asleep in bed. I wanted to sleep but I was always too hyped up from work. It took time to wind down. Eventually, I slipped into sleep, only to be woken up the next morning to do it all over again. This continued for about two years. We were happy together, but this wasn't the life we wanted.

...

The life we were living wasn't sustainable. JoAnne and I were working ourselves to death. We welcomed a second son, Cole, into our family in the spring of 1983. JoAnne continued to watch kids while managing the added chaos of a newborn. I continued to work exorbitant hours at DB's. Nine months later, just two days before Christmas, we sold the mobile home and purchased a house in Sunnyside.

It was a cute house—just shy of nine hundred square feet with three bedrooms and one bathroom—on top of a hill on Riverside Drive. The lot to the west was empty, so we had a great view of the valley. The kids also had plenty of space to play. We were able to afford our mortgage, but our other expenses made finances tight. As a result, we cut corners so we could afford to live.

That first winter, we disconnected the oil furnace—a grease-stained, oil-guzzling cylinder—and waited for an alternative heating source to be delivered. And delivered it was. One afternoon a flatbed semi-truck backed its way onto the grass on the west side of the house. It dumped massive delimbed logs in the yard next to the carport. We cut those logs into usable firewood and used them to heat the house throughout the winter. While the firewood did indeed save us money, it had its downsides. No matter how hot the fire's blaze was before bed, we were always awakened by a chill in the night. It forced me out of my blankets to restart the fire. Unfortunately, the wood stove was down the hall in the living room. No matter how quickly I relit the fire, it always took some time to stop shivering once I returned to bed. Despite these midnight rekindling efforts, there were numerous mornings we awoke to ice frozen *inside* the windowpanes. JoAnne and I slept in a heated waterbed at the time. More often than not, the small bodies of our two boys found their way across the hall and into bed alongside ours. These are memories I will cherish forever.

By the next spring we were finally settled in. Every week JoAnne and I replayed the same conversation as we tried to figure out a better option. Besides having each other and the boys, everything else seemed to be caving in around us. There is a reason why they call it the daily grind. We were being crushed by the weight of the work required to feed our little family.

On an ordinary afternoon, JoAnne approached me with the idea that would change our lives. We were discussing our predicament yet again and our hopes for the future. I had been in the restaurant business now for four years. It hadn't taken more than a few months to realize it was not what I wanted to be doing for the rest of my life. The job stability persuaded me to stay even though I was depressed and run down. I did what was required to provide for my family.

We replayed our 'what can we do' conversation yet again, when out of the blue, JoAnne said, "What do you think about getting involved in sales?"

I had always been intrigued by finance and I felt my biggest asset was my people skills. But where would I go?

She continued, "My mom and dad are living over in Germany. My dad knows some guys who have a company there. Why don't you get your securities license? Let's move. You could do financial consulting over in Germany."

My eyebrows receded up my forehead like a bad hairline. Was she serious? The suggestion caught me off-guard. Like most people respond to radical change, I rejected it. That wasn't going to work for so many reasons.

Recognizing the Spirit

In order to make a dramatic life change, I needed some definitive revelation from God. Fortunately, I had quite a bit of experience learning how to recognize the Spirit from my mission a handful of years before.

I spent the first half of my missionary service in the Denver, Colorado mission, but due to boundary realignment I spent the last half in the Independence, Missouri mission. I felt the purpose in moving me to the new mission was to implement the lesson about recognizing the Spirit. When people knew how to identify the Spirit in their life, we noticed a tremendous increase in their desire to follow Christ's example and be baptized. That lesson had really taken a hold of me. I gained a reputation for teaching with the Spirit. I wanted to help other missionaries see how it helped people accept the gospel of Jesus Christ.

My new mission president had his hands full managing the merging of five missions. He was bombarded by a plethora of Elders advising him on what he should incorporate from their previous mission cultures. I was among them. I approached President Johnson about the lesson. His response was less animated than my delivery. He said he needed to think it over and continue to run things as they were for now. It was a gracious rejection, but I wasn't about to let it go. Besides the fact that rejection always tends to spur me on, I *knew* this helped people. So, I continued to teach people how to recognize the Spirit before teaching them anything else. I also taught the lesson to any other missionary who would listen.

I received a call from President Johnson a few weeks later. He extended an invitation to serve as one of his traveling assistants. My new companion and I traveled the mission, trained other missionaries, and assisted the president. I knew this was my chance to spread the inspired 'Recognizing the Spirit' lesson to the entire mission.

Unfortunately, it was not meant to be. That week a group of missionaries in Topeka got into trouble and needed to be separated. This left the president in a tough spot. Transfers had just occurred a few days before and everyone was settling into their new assignments. Now, because of these Elders' behavior, almost everyone had to be shuffled around again. I knew what I could do to help prevent that. I approached President Johnson in his office as he stared at the transfer board. I offered to serve the Topeka zone and help straighten everything out. He agreed to my proposal and in less than a week I switched assignments and moved twice.

...

I spent five wonderful months serving the people in Topeka. I loved my assignment, but I felt more apprehensive with each passing day. I thought the Lord wanted me to implement the 'Recognizing the Spirit' lesson to this mission. Yet, my time as a missionary was coming to a close. Only two months remained before I would travel home to Washington. At this time, I received a second call from the mission president to be his assistant.

A few weeks later, the leaders in the mission gathered to be trained. As part of this all-day training, my new companion, Elder Walpole, and I were given time to instruct. With little time remaining as a missionary, I knew this was my last chance to share my message. It seemed meant to be. In the days leading up to the conference, I taught Elder Walpole the 'Recognizing the Spirit' lesson. I shared with him my feelings about being called to this mission and position for the purpose of sharing it.

The day of the conference arrived. The room was full of Elders from around the mission seated in rows of folding chairs. We listened to the other trainings until, finally, the time was ours. We arranged four chairs in the front of the room. President Johnson and another Elder played the role of individuals learning about the Church of Jesus Christ of Latter-Day Saints. Elder Walpole and I cracked open our Bibles and read scriptures that explained some of the roles of the Spirit — which included bringing comfort and teaching truth. I shared that for me, the Spirit most often felt like an impression, or a good idea that I felt not only in my mind, but also in my heart.

After our training, President Johnson dismissed everyone for lunch. He approached Elder Walpole and me and told us he was impressed by what he had experienced. He asked us to write up the lesson and distribute it to all the missionaries. We were also assigned to travel and demonstrate the lesson throughout the mission.

My last six weeks of missionary service were the sweetest. Elder Walpole and I instructed missionaries how to teach with the Spirit and how to help others recognize the Spirit of God in their lives. Learning to recognize the Spirit led others to Jesus more effectively than any other method I knew. It filled me with immense joy to witness others grow closer to Christ. Not only because people changed their lives for the better, but also because I knew God had worked through me to accomplish His purposes.

Several years later, my cousin Robyn was called to serve in the same Independence, Missouri mission. Years after her return, we were reminiscing about the people and places we had both grown to love. Out of curiosity, I asked her if the missionaries were still using the lesson about recognizing the Spirit. Her eyes lit up. She told me it was funny I had asked, because she used that lesson often, with great success. It made such an impact in her teaching that other missionaries asked her what she was doing. She advised them to help people recognize the Spirit in their life using the lesson I introduced. I smiled and my eyes brimmed with tears.

. . .

Over the next year I entertained the idea of moving to Germany. In the evenings I took the suggestion out and examined it from every angle to determine its worth. More importantly, God began to soften my heart. I tried to put off my concerns and began to listen for the Spirit. I was willing to take a leap of faith into the unknown if that was what the Lord wanted.

After months of mental tug-of-war, I realized that we had to make a change in order to change our lives. Maybe moving to Germany could lead to the life we wanted for our family. There were so many unknowns, but one thing I did come to believe was that nothing was going to happen for us unless we took control. So, I finally decided to do it. I would get my securities license and we would move to Germany.

As soon as I made the decision, the storm inside me calmed. I approached the Lord in prayer and asked Him whether the decision I made was the right one. It was then—and only then—the Spirit spoke through my feelings: *this is what you need to do.* I told JoAnne. She looked relieved. Together, we began to prepare to leave the United States.

Part Two

Faith Precedes the Miracle

I sat in my last interview with President Lambourne before the mission split working up the courage to follow through with a spiritual prompting. A few minutes into the interview, I steeled myself.

"President?" I said, my face full of concern.

"Yes, Elder Van Leuven?"

"I wanted to let you know that my right leg has been giving me trouble."

I looked at the ground and tried to keep my voice even, "It is beginning to atrophy like my arms did before I came out on my mission." After a short pause, I continued, "I've been praying about it and I was instructed by the Spirit to ask you for a blessing." My blue eyes flitted up and stared earnestly into his. "Through the power of the Priesthood, I know you can heal me."

An involuntary, "*Whoa*," escaped his lips. President Lambourne sat quietly for a minute as he absorbed what I had said. Eventually, he said, "I'm going to need some time to think about the blessing." Instead of returning to the mission home in Denver that night, President Lambourne reserved a hotel room in Dodge City. He planned to fast and pray the rest of the evening to prepare to give me a blessing the next day.

The next morning, my heart pounded as I stood outside the hotel door with my missionary companion. I was slightly nauseous as I reached forward and knocked on the door. President Lambourne invited us in. Inside were four other missionaries who worked closely with the president. There was a nervous energy in the room as I took a seat on a chair in the middle of the room. Then, the men encircled me and laid their hands on my head.

President Lambourne called me by name. "In the name of Jesus Christ," he said, "I rebuke the disease from your body and command it to depart."

I felt an electric wave begin in the soles of my feet. It slowly migrated up my ankles, through my legs and into my abdomen. The current continued upward through my chest, arms and neck. Finally, it seemed to go up through my head and into the hands of the men encircling me. The entire process lasted only a matter of seconds, but I was forever changed. God had healed my body of muscular dystrophy. I *felt* it.

Barriers

As with any life-altering decision, the decision to move was difficult to make, but we had finally decided. Our decision gave us direction. We were moving to Germany. While it felt like a journey to reach our decision, it was only the beginning of the long road ahead. We had planned to put down roots in Sunnyside and had only owned our home for a year. We had moved before, but this was more than moving to a new city—we were leaving the country. It was something neither of us had done before.

There were many things to consider as we prepared to leave. A consequence of taking so long to decide was that during the year of indecision, JoAnne became pregnant with our third child. This made leaving both harder and easier. Harder, because we would have to leave our insurance through the restaurant when we moved. We were unsure of what to do when the baby finally came or how we would pay for it all. JoAnne's pregnancy also made the decision easier because I knew our growing family needed more than what our current situation could provide. We were going to have to make a drastic change if we wanted a better life. If we were brave enough to take the leap, I trusted God would catch us.

We began to tell people. Most looked at us like we were crazy—many commented as much. Perhaps they thought we had our midlife crisis a few decades too early. Who could blame them? It *was* a radical shift in our plan, but it felt inspired. The hardest people to tell were my parents. They also lived in Sunnyside and we saw them often. JoAnne frequently took the kids to visit in the evenings or on weekends when I worked. Not only did our new plan mean moving ourselves away, but it also meant taking away our two boys—their only grandchildren. This move also meant they would miss the birth and infancy of their next grandchild. To say they were not happy with our decision would be an understatement.

The next big step had been in progress for a number of months—I had to become certified as a financial consultant. Because reading was a challenge for me, the process was excruciating. I spent hours upon hours studying investment risk, taxation, equity and debt instruments, securities, options, retirement, and mutual funds. The state exam was easy—I passed the first time without a problem. But my Series 7 test was a different story.

There were several timed tests—covering different areas of finance—each with their own fees. Without fail, I was the last person in the room when the clock ran out. The first time, I was devastated to learn I had not passed. It was not because I didn't know the answers. It took me too long to figure out what the questions were asking, causing me to run out of time before finishing. After multiple attempts, I developed a system to help me. It became like a game—with every question, I eliminated the two obviously wrong choices so I wouldn't waste time re-reading them. Then, I focused on the remaining choices and decided from there. Failing the tests the first time around was both a shot to my confidence and my wallet, but I wasn't going to let it stop me. In fact, it motivated me to keep trying until I succeeded.

Thankfully, being open with people about our new journey brought good news as well. JoAnne's father helped me get in contact with a father-son team who sold insurance in Germany. After months of communication, they extended me a job offer. I signed a contract to start work at the end of July. With a job secured, our plan began to take shape.

A sweet, Latina woman in her fifties—who worked as a hostess at the restaurant with me—was interested in our home. After touring the house, she made an offer. We had to get creative with the deal due to her lack of funds for a down payment, coupled with our short timeline. We drafted up an agreement; we would get $1,000 as a down payment in July. Meanwhile, JoAnne and I would continue to carry the mortgage into the winter. At the end of November, she would pay us another $3,000 and we would refinance the house into her name. We were relieved to sell our house and happy to help a coworker buy her own.

For me, the hardest part of moving to Germany was selling my two collector cars. The cars—a 1954 Austin Healey and a 1971 Challenger convertible—were like my babies. They were both acquired in those early years of our marriage with funds from a good stock pick.

The Austin Healey was a steal of a deal from a gentleman who squirreled it away in his garage for years. With the help of a friend, I fixed it up. The only part of the Austin Healey original to the name was the body; everything else on the two-seater sports car had been added over time to convert it into a street rod. In fact, when my friend and I finished fixing it up, it resembled a Ford Cobra. It was fun to drive—stomping on the gas even brought the front end of the car up!

When I bought the Challenger, it was an ugly orange. Another friend helped me sand it down and repaint the body a beautiful Cadillac pearl white. That car was *classy*. One time, I even led a town parade with the honorary person riding in back of the convertible. As soon as I listed it for sale, I was immediately contacted by a man in Seattle who wanted to fly out and buy it. The motor needed some work, but he bought it and drove back to Seattle. While I made a profit from both cars, to watch each of them go was painful, like a piece of my heart went with them. Selling those cars was a great personal sacrifice, but it had to be done to finance our move.

...

When I was little, my uncle took my siblings and me for rides across the fields in his little prop plane. He even let me fly it once when I was older. I had only been on two commercial flights before—to and from my mission. When I arrived at the airport to fly to Germany, I was overwhelmed by the largeness of it all. Here I was, a little farm boy from Washington, about to fly across the world to live in a foreign country. A country whose only history I knew from what I had learned in school about World War II. It was the biggest undertaking of my life and I was out of my element.

I landed in Amsterdam and was warned to keep my luggage close if I wanted to keep it. I stood in the train station struggling to read the transfer board. Thankfully, a stranger took pity on me. He helped me discover I was in the wrong area altogether. He then directed me to the train headed for Germany.

I tried to wrap my brain around the fact that I was halfway around the world from where I had spent my entire life. It left me feeling slightly dizzy, but perhaps that was the jetlag. Either way, I found a seat on the correct train and fell asleep. However, I was soon woken up by a man's hand in my pocket.

"Hey! What are you doing?" I asked, as I sat up and scooted away.

The man shrugged it off, but I knew he tried to steal from me. I got up and found a different seat for the remainder of the journey.

After two days of travel, I finally made it to Mainz. We had talked about it for so long; it was surreal to finally be in Germany. The next morning—my first full day in Germany—I went to start my new job.

Although nervous, the sun was shining and I felt energized about this new prospect for my family. JoAnne's dad went with me to make the introductions. I was grateful he was there to help me find the building because I was unable to speak or read in German yet. We entered the building and were directed to the office of the father and son with whom I had been communicating. After short introductions, they looked at me and said, "I'm sorry. We folded the company. We're moving back to the United States."

What? I must not have heard correctly. Yet, the father assured me that I had. Things had been rough for their business for a while. It was time to cut their losses and move back to the United States. There was no job for me here.

I felt like a dark blanket had been wrapped around my head. There wasn't enough oxygen to breathe.

That night I laid awake in bed for hours. My body was exhausted, but I was unable to turn off my mind. The job was gone. I had traveled halfway around the world and the job was *gone*. There were a few things I knew.

One: I was 5,000 miles away from home.

Two: I had a pregnant wife and two toddlers scheduled to move here in six weeks.

Three: we sold *everything* for this job, and now it was gone. There was nothing to go back to.

I also knew I had felt the Spirit urge us to pursue this opportunity. I didn't know what was going on. How could I have gotten it so wrong? I questioned God: *Isn't this what You wanted?*

What were we going to do now?

Where is the Kitchen?

I was understandably angry at what had happened. Not only that the company led me on for months, but that they waited until I had moved across the world to break the news to me. How do you respond to something like that? Thankfully, I kept my wits about me and had the good sense to ask a few follow-up questions instead of reacting the way I wanted to. I inquired after their notable competitors in the area. When they responded with a few names, I jumped at the opportunity to get the competitors' contact information. Within the hour I had set up an appointment to meet with another consulting company.

Over the next few days, I prayed incessantly as I waited for my interview with the competing company. I was trying to pave a way forward while simultaneously calculating if there was any possible way to go back to the States. JoAnne was still there with the boys, after all. If I could scrounge up the money to make it home, I may be able to convince my old boss to take me back. We could figure out the living situation from there. Perhaps there was still a way to back out of this royal mistake. Yet, if there was, I couldn't seem to find it. I wanted to go home, but the money wasn't there. Like a small boat taking on water in a stormy sea, I was trying everything to keep from capsizing. Eventually, the feeling came over me: *this is where you need to be.* The sentence played over and over in my mind. Though I didn't know how it would be possible, I clung to the hope that things would work out.

Within the week, I was hired for my first financial consulting job. I worked in an office with twenty other guys in Frankfurt. The small operation worked under a larger umbrella company in Brussels. The job required use of the state-of-the-art TRS-80—an all-in-one computer monitor unit with a small screen on the top half, floppy disk reader on the right and built-in keyboard. With all the new aspects of the job, I was grateful not to have to learn how to type on the thing. I had cute girls in high school to thank for that. Not them directly, but rather, because of them I signed up for a typing class in high school. Thankfully, I learned to type fairly well before I was eventually kicked out of the class.

With work secured, I hunted for reliable transportation and a place to live. It made sense for us to live with JoAnne's parents until we got our feet on the ground. Her parents had been living in Germany doing genealogy work for the church and already had an apartment. However, we wanted to find a bigger place to fit us all.

There were certain things I assumed when it came to renting. I didn't realize all that I took for granted until I walked into a house without a kitchen. Imagine my surprise during a home tour when I walked into the room where the kitchen was *supposed* to be only to find four walls and exposed plumbing. The idea was as bizarre to me as a face without a nose. The first time, I thought it was a fluke. By the second apartment, I was asking questions. Apparently, each tenant bought a customized kitchen setup for their rental. Although it surely would not fit in their next kitchen space properly, the previous tenant always took theirs with them!

I eventually found a four-story townhouse in the city of Mainz-Kastel. Now that we had a place to live, we still had to find and install an entire kitchen! JoAnne's parents moved their belongings into the top floor while I chased down a used kitchen. With each kitchen being customized to a specific home, it was difficult to find a used cabinetry set that would fit into our empty room. Finally, one was secured with most of our remaining funds. It seemed like every spare minute was used to put that room together before my family's arrival. JoAnne's dad was an enormous help. He hauled in the cabinetry and appliances and adjusted things as we installed them to make it all fit properly in the new space. We felt the pressure of dwindling time. I knew if the house was not ready to live in, JoAnne would have a meltdown when she finally arrived. I wouldn't blame her. Fortunately, we finished just in time.

...

JoAnne and the boys made it to Germany without incident. It was a superhuman feat. I don't know how she managed the luggage along with both boys and a large pregnant belly on the lengthy flight. I couldn't have done it. I met them at the airport in Amsterdam. I was overjoyed to see my family after the longest separation JoAnne and I had experienced in our six years of marriage. I gestured at our new ride to my exhausted wife. The car was a faded yellow Opel Ascona—Europe's version of a four-door sedan. After loading everything and everyone into the car, we made the journey to our new home.

In the car, JoAnne slipped her feet out of her shoes. The flight had caused them to swell. Her typically dainty toes resembled stuffed sausages. As she moved her feet back and forth, we could see the water wave left to right.

...

Everything was different in Germany. We had to adjust to an entirely new culture. JoAnne came home from the market one day incredulous at her experience there. When she entered a little grocery store, she was greeted by a pyramid of red apples. She began to pick apples from the stack when suddenly, an older woman began to chastise her in German. JoAnne froze. She eventually figured out she was not allowed to select her own fruit. She told the attendant how many she wanted—fünf Stück—and the apples were retrieved for her. It was explained in striking tones that she couldn't pick her own because *someone had to have the bruised ones.* To her dismay, over the years it seemed like that *someone* was nearly always her.

...

We attended church with the American servicemen in Wiesbaden. It was ideal because the services were held in English. There were many young couples in the congregation who also had small children. It seemed fertile ground for friendship. However, it proved difficult for us to make friends there. While we were American like them, we didn't share their second major trait—military service. People were kind, but little interactions continued to remind us of our outsider position. For example, one Sunday during the Sacrament meeting, I was asked to stand for a sustaining vote to become the ward mission leader. During the procedural raising of hands, one brother with bright red hair, Clyde Dowdage, stood and said, "What? What! This guy can't be the ward mission leader! He's not even airborne!" His remarks were followed by bouts of laughter from the other families in the congregation. I quickly took my seat as a crimson heat rash worked its way up from under my white collar.

...

Sometimes in life we hear something that resonates with us so deeply, it influences the way we live from that point onward. One such phrase that has always stuck with me was when President Thomas S. Monson said, "It's better to break a rule than to break a heart." With the delivery of our third child, we were startled to find out—when translated into German—the phrase can become, "It's better to break a rule than to let someone shoplift."

JoAnne had been in Germany for five weeks when she went into labor on her due date. I remember it was a Saturday. With two kids already, we felt like we knew what to expect. However, much like my surprise with the kitchenless apartments, we were caught off guard by the lack of accommodations at the hospital. When we arrived, we learned they did not provide sheets, a pillow or even towels for the delivery. JoAnne also needed to supply her own gown because they did not have anything for her to wear. Of course, we were also responsible for diapers and clothing the baby. We were supposed to have brought everything we could possibly need, but we stood there empty handed. JoAnne's mother was able to run to the market for the essentials while JoAnne was admitted. Her mother was gone for quite a while, but she returned with the necessary items and a story to share:

She raced around the market and was standing in line with her items as the bell announced twelve o'clock. On

Saturdays, the markets closed at noon. At the last chime of the bell, it was announced that the store was now closed. She would have to leave without the items in her basket. Luckily, she was a feisty woman and quickly replied in German, "Okay, that's fine. My daughter is in labor at the hospital. I will walk out the door, but I'm taking these things with me."

The clerk was shocked by her brazen disregard for the rules and immediately responded, "Oh no! I'll help you."

"I thought you would."

The clerk let her pay for the items before leaving.

Our two boys had been delivered in the States via cesarean section. Although it was rather unusual in those days, our next child was delivered naturally. We were grateful everything had gone smoothly as we stared at the newest member of our family—a tiny, pink girl. We examined her again and again. She was perfect, but she still needed a name.

My dad's name was Myles C Van Leuven. Not 'C' with a period; the 'C' was not short for anything, it was just 'C'. My parents named me Martin C Van Leuven. Again, the 'C' didn't stand for anything.

When JoAnne and I started having kids we decided to continue the tradition in our own way. We named our firstborn Myles Craig, after my father. This gave him the same initials as my father and me. As an adult, he goes by Myles, but we called him Craig when he was little. We named our second son Martin Cole, but his entire life he has gone by Cole.

For a girl, I had always liked the name Nisha. Unfortunately, that didn't go along with our MC initials. After talking it over, we decided to name her Misha (which means Michael in Russian). We looked at her, and the name fit. We were instantly in love with our sweet Misha Christine.

As evening approached, the nurse took Misha into the nursery to allow JoAnne to rest. A few hours later, JoAnne woke up and wanted to nurse, so I went to find Misha. To our alarm, I found the nursery locked, with no adult in sight. I could see Misha through the glass, but I couldn't get to her. We spent the first night in the hospital trying to figure out how to get to our only daughter.

Hours later, we learned that the nursing staff only went to the nursery every four hours to feed the babies. The next evening, JoAnne refused to let them take Misha. A strong believer that you cannot spoil a baby with too much love, JoAnne wanted to keep her close. Misha was our baby, after all, and we wanted to be there for her when she needed us.

Taking Misha home was one of the scariest events of my life. I wasn't scared of the physical act of driving her to our shared row house, but of the realities that faced us there. In the hospital, we were able to bask in the miracle of our new child and forget—if only for a moment—the dire situation in which we found ourselves in Germany.

Things were not going well at work. I was having difficulty finding clients. In a sales job, no clients meant no income. Our move to Germany was supposed to be the solution to our money problems, but we were even worse off than before. It seemed we had bet everything on a losing horse.

Our Last Twenty Marks

We arrived in Germany with our suitcases and the clothes on our backs. The plan was to buy what we needed for the baby once we were settled. The only problem was that once we were in Germany, we no longer had any money for clothes.

Misha had exactly two outfits: a pink dress edged in white lace from the bishop's wife, and a white flowered shirt worn under a dusty pink velour onesie with snaps on the shoulder. Those two outfits rarely lasted longer than a few hours. Without convenient access to a washer and dryer, it was impossible to keep her clothes clean. Because of this, she nearly always wore her older brothers' shirts, knotted at the bottom. She didn't have a baby blanket, so we wrapped her in regular sized blankets. I know she was an infant and didn't know the difference, but we were ashamed.

Before we knew it, it was October and we decided not to bless Misha in church yet. JoAnne was still healing from the delivery and I was scrambling for more clients at work. It was the beginning of the month and our bills were due. We were hurting. Our savings was already spent. We did not know what else to do. I was stressed out to the point of depression and was also spiritually drained. I took the duty of providing for my family very seriously. Not being able to afford clothing for Misha left me feeling unworthy to bless her.

A month passed and we thought more about Misha's baby blessing. We planned to dress her in the pink dress given to us by the bishop's wife. JoAnne told me we needed to buy tights and a slip in order to bless Misha in November. I turned out my pocket. I had twenty marks—equaling about seven US dollars. Money in hand, JoAnne went to the coble-stoned plaza where the stores were located. There she bought a slip and tights with the last of our money.

Our circumstances should have led us to ask for assistance from the church, but we honestly didn't consider it as an option. Even with JoAnne's father in the bishopric—or perhaps in part because of it—we didn't ask. Church assistance did not feel like it was meant for us. We had both been raised on the meager salaries of schoolteachers. If our parents could do it, so could we. Besides, I couldn't bring myself to ask for financial assistance when I was supposed to be helping others manage their own finances. I was too ashamed. Looking back, we should have asked for help; we desperately needed it. Perhaps I let my pride get in the way. Whatever the reason, those feelings kept us from seeking help. Thankfully, the Lord saw fit to help us anyway.

A knock on the door caught both JoAnne and me at home one afternoon. A young mother stood on the porch with two bulging shopping bags. JoAnne greeted her sister's friend, Donna Pahl, and invited her in. A rosy glow crept over her cheeks as she said, "I don't know why I'm here."

After an awkward pause, she started to explain, "My daughter is the first child born in our family. There are no other children in either of our families and my parents send us clothes like crazy. Friends and relatives also send them. Honestly, my goal each day is to get my daughter to wear each outfit at least once before she outgrows them. There's just so much." She held up the bags. "So, I brought over some things. Is there any way you could use them?"

I looked in surprise from Donna to JoAnne, who had tears running down her face. Donna Pahl did not know how dire our situation was. We had not told anyone. Yet, here she was, an angel with grocery bags of clothes for wings.

JoAnne nodded and said, "Thank you. I know we can use these." After a tearful exchange, Donna Pahl left.

God had not forgotten us. Although we were strangers in a foreign land, He remembered us. This experience lifted our spirits. It walked us back from the edge of despair—even though we still had no money to speak of. We eventually became desperate enough to call home for help.

It had taken going hungry a few times to humble me enough to ask my parents and siblings for money. But the day finally came when I could not put it off any longer. JoAnne and the kids needed more than I could give them. With them in mind, I went to our bedroom and shut the door. I sat down at the desk and made the long-distance call.

First, I called my older brother Kirk. Unfortunately, things were tight for him as well; he had no money to lend. I sat for a few minutes after the call and steeled myself for the next one. Picking up the telephone once more, I dialed the familiar number.

"Hello?" my dad's voice answered.

I took a deep breath and told my dad about our precarious situation. Until now, we had avoided telling people back home how bad things were. We didn't want them to worry. Now, we had no other option. Sadly, my mom's health was deteriorating while her medical bills continued to accumulate. I thanked my dad for taking the call and hung up the phone dejectedly. The last flutter of hope inside me went still. There was no money coming to save us.

We put the kids to bed that night and JoAnne could tell something was wrong. My eyes were on my lap as we sat down together. I told her I had called home. With a trembling voice I broke the news that no one had any money to send. The air became heavy as the words left my lips. My eyes flitted upward. It shattered my heart to see her face fall. There is nothing quite so tragic as the loss of hope. We cried together for some time.

"What are we going to do?" she asked.

We discussed going back to America. Regrettably, it was not a viable option: traveling required money. Without money, we were stuck in Germany. What's more, we still felt the pull to be there. God sent us across an entire ocean; there must be a purpose behind it—beyond us going hungry, that is. I constantly sought out new clients, but those first few months had not produced much for my efforts. The unfortunate reality of life is that oftentimes, the fruit is needed the moment the seed is planted.

During this period of spiritual and financial depression, I had to hold tightly to my previous faith-building experiences to keep me going. As I tried to remember that God had worked miracles in my life before, it helped me dare to hope He would do so again. One such experience that kept me going happened when I was a missionary.

In Kansas, the land is so flat that they call molehills mountains. The landscape lays in stark contrast to Washington's towering mountains and evergreens. A somewhat unique consequence of the horizontal scenery is the ability to see things coming from miles away: especially the weather.

One of the more difficult parts of missionary work was trying to find new people to teach. Sometimes, we combined efforts to help other missionaries make new contacts. On one such occasion, many of us gathered outside the home of a pair of sister missionaries. The plan was to split up and talk to people in the street, knock doors, and meet new people for them to teach. Unfortunately, as we all arrived at the house, the sky began to drizzle. In the distance, we could see a wall of rain approaching.

I was deflated. We had already spent the time to get everyone there. I could smell discouragement in the wind. I knew the rain would make it harder for everyone to work seriously. It was going to be an opportunity wasted. Yet, amid these negative thoughts came another: *you need to use the priesthood and command it to stop raining.* What a strange thought. I shrugged it off. I had never done anything like that before. Soon the thought returned: *use the priesthood to command the clouds.* I began to question if it was the Spirit prompting me to act. After a third nudge, I decided it was a prompting. I needed to stop second guessing and act.

I walked around the corner of the tiny white house for some privacy. Once alone, I squared my right arm and commanded the rain to depart. To my amazement, the blanket of clouds immediately began to break up. Before my eyes, the dark, menacing wall of rain transformed into puffy, white cotton. The day was beautiful, and our purpose was fulfilled.

As I knelt beside my bed that night, I thanked Heavenly Father for allowing me to have such a dramatic faith-promoting experience. During my prayer, I again felt prompted. This time, the Spirit impressed upon me: *command the weather to go back to its original state.* It did not take three nudges for me to respond this time. I raised my arm and quietly commanded the weather to go back to its original state. As soon as the words left my lips, lightning lit up the room. Bellowing claps of thunder soon followed and rain poured from the heavens onto our roof and into the streets. My eyes were likewise overflowing with joy. I was overwhelmed by the experience and evidence that God heard me.

. . .

Amid our financial drought in Germany, I frequently pleaded with God for assistance—for miracles. It was only fall and we desperately wanted to give up. We told ourselves that if we could make it to winter and collect the money from the house sale, everything would be okay. Honestly, we didn't know if we could last one more day.

Misha was only a few weeks old and we had come up short, again. There was not enough money to buy food that night. I remember pleading, "Lord, I need help."

After the prayer I had the idea: *you need to go down to Barmer Insurance.* It was an extremely random thought, but it felt like the Spirit. So, I walked out to my yellow Ascona and drove to the insurance building. Once in the building, I followed the arrowed Barmer sign that led to a smoked glass window. Still unsure of what I was doing, I opened the door. Two people stood as I entered the narrow office space. My ability to converse in German was extremely limited, so I asked, "Entshuldingung bitte, sprechen sie Englisch?" (Excuse me please, do you speak English?)

A smiling woman stepped forward to talk with me. "Why are you here?" she asked in a thick accent.

The truth? God told me to go there. "I don't know why I'm here..." I found myself responding. "My name is Martin Van Leuven," I added, a bit uncomfortably—as if that would help.

Her eyes lit up with recognition. "Herr Van Loyfen?" (Her accent changed the sound of my name.)

"Yeah..." I said, confused by her sudden excitement.

Her smile widened. "We've been looking and looking and looking for you!" She grabbed something from the desk behind her and handed it to me. "Here are five hundred marks for the birth of your child."

I stared at the money. "For the birth of my child? What do you mean?"

She explained that to incentivize people to raise the German birth rate, the government paid people to have children. "So, because you are on our insurance, you get five hundred marks for the birth of your child. Congratulations!"

I stared at the money in my palm. By the time I made it to the car, tears were running down my face. That money tided us over until it was time to collect the payment for the house that winter.

. . .

Occasionally, my body tries to show me who's boss. One night I walked from the garage to our home. Ours was the first in a long string of row houses that lined both sides of the street. As I reached the screen door, my right leg buckled; it just gave out. Without warning, I fell face-first into the opaque glass. A roar like dropped silverware filled my head as it fractured the door. The black wire mesh embedded in the glass kept my head from going through the glass. Instead, my chin slammed into the ground and split open, which forced me to go to the emergency room for stitches.

I checked my watch as the doctor sewed me up and wrapped a white gauze bandage around my head. As soon as he finished, I was out of there. I had an appointment to keep with a prospective client. Had we been in a better financial position, I may have been tempted to reschedule. Instead, I ran through my sales pitch once more as I drove to his house. All the while, I tried to ignore the throbbing in my face.

He opened the door and exclaimed, "What happened to your face?"

"Oh, you just have to ignore me. I fell and got hurt." I stepped into the house and continued, "But, I told you I'd come out and visit with you, so I'm here." I walked away from the encounter that night with a new client.

...

It was nearing Christmas when JoAnne and I became concerned. The $3,000 payment from my coworker for our house in Sunnyside was overdue. We had agreed to a date in November, but the day came and went without a word. We were upset, but not yet alarmed. Perhaps it was in the mail on its way to us at that very moment. Our concern grew to distress however, after two weeks went by without being able to contact her. Desperate, I called my old restaurant and tried to catch her at work. I found out she had quit her job, and no one had seen her. My stomach plummeted.

Bill, an old friend from work, went to check on the house for me. He called back with alarming news. As he described the home, I could see it in my mind's eye: I was standing in the kitchen staring at large empty spaces where the appliances once stood. I saw the broken toilet bowl in the bathroom. The house that had so recently been our home was trashed. I felt violated.

JoAnne and I were at a loss. Emotionally, we had been pushing ourselves to hold out for that money. We were like runners who had trained for a 10k only to discover they were running a marathon. It was too much for us to handle. We desperately needed the funds and now we would never see a penny. Even worse, the house was no longer in a condition to be rented.

Unsure of what to do, I called an attorney. I wanted to avoid damaging our credit. We didn't have any money to fix it up and it would not sell as it was. At the attorney's suggestion, I contacted the mortgage lender and signed the house over to the bank. We walked away from our first real home like a bad breakup: broken-hearted and a little more wary of the world.

The Little Yellow Car

It was in this desperate plight that things finally began to turn around at work. A large, dark-haired Italian named Joe D'Atilia was a phenomenal senior sales representative. In fact, he was the highest performing sales representative in the entire company for many years. Joe understood sales better than anyone I ever met. He didn't just talk the talk; he walked the walk.

Joe must have seen something in me because he decided to take me under his wing. We went on several sales calls together where he broadened my sales understanding. He saw to every aspect of the pitch and taught me not only how to approach a sale, but also *why* I was supposed to approach it that way. And his techniques worked! I was eager to learn and received permission to record his presentations. Later, at home, I tried my best to mirror his approaches. I had learned on my mission that mirroring strong techniques brings success.

By the beginning of the new year, my hope began to revive ever so slightly. With Joe as my mentor, maybe I could scrape together a living for us. But I knew it took more time and effort than I currently had to give. I found that I could say and do all the right things, but without a polished charismatic touch, the pitch fell flat every time. I needed to spend more time perfecting my technique if we were going to make it. This led me to have a heart-to-heart with JoAnne. I told her I thought I could turn things around for us, but as my partner, I needed her support. If she could manage the mountainous task of managing the house and kids, I would spend my time doing everything I could to become a better salesman: I would provide. Never one to back down from a challenge, she agreed. With my wife and I on the same page, (along with Joe's mentorship) I began to see some improvements in my abilities. This, thankfully, directly translated to our bank account.

...

American military housing was full of single men and young families with stable jobs who spoke English. This was where I finally found my niche. The way our business was set up, if I could provide evidence of a new military client, I received an advance on my pay before the client contributed any funds. All I needed was an allotment slip showing the client had signed over money to come out of their next paycheck. They were the ideal clients. The only problem with this setup was I wasn't allowed to solicit in their neighborhoods. All salesmen needed special permits to solicit in the military housing communities and the company I worked for did not have clearance. Not willing to let my family starve, I began to sneak into the military housing neighborhoods to sell insurance and securities anyway.

It's surprising what you will do to survive. The first time I was caught soliciting in military housing without a permit, I was embarrassed to be escorted out by military police. It felt like being caught stealing cookies from the jar. However, it quickly became normal. The only punishment was to be escorted out of the neighborhood, which wasn't much of a deterrent. It got to the point where after I was escorted out, I watched the officers walk away, then sneaked back in to continue selling.

I remember nights in the dead of winter when I stood outside waiting for guys to get home from work. When they finally showed up, I said, "Oh, hey. I was in the area and stopped by to pick up that allotment slip from you." Once that paper was in my hand, I could go home knowing we had enough money to buy food.

The most pivotal door I ever knocked was in one of those military communities. I had been working the area for a while—we'd been in Germany nearly six months— and determined it was in my best interest to seek out officers. Not only did they tend to be more stable clients, but I also made more commission on each sale because they made more money. I was in an area I had been kicked out of multiple times before when I approached a door in the back corner of a row of townhomes. It was already dark, and I was losing steam. At the time, I didn't know this would be the door to a better future.

As the door opened, a man filled the lighted doorway. Right away I could tell this guy was somebody important; he had a commanding demeanor. I explained who I was and what I did. He brushed me off by saying his finances were already taken care of. However, we visited on the doorstep for a few minutes longer. When I learned he had a son, I asked if he had ever thought about setting up a college savings account for him. This question seemed to catch him off guard. After a pause, he softened and said, "Yeah, that's a pretty good idea." He didn't have time that evening but invited me back.

During our second visit I set up a college investment account for his son. Before I left, I asked if he knew any other officers in his unit that I could help. He referred me to several friends nearby. I went home rejoicing at one of my first big sales, still unaware at the significance of this encounter. You see, my luck began to turn after our meeting. Being a full-bird colonel, Mr. Wallis had tremendous influence on the other servicemen: he was the head honcho, if you will. For some reason, Colonel Wallis decided to back me. I had impressed him with my financial knowledge, and he said, "I'm going to help you out." And he did.

Once he gave the nod, others began to trust me. It became known that I was Colonel Wallis' financial adviser. Over the following months, I received numerous referrals from people who knew and respected Colonel Wallis—and many of their friends as well. Through these successful sales, I gained confidence and perfected my technique.

...

When I moved to Germany, I bought my yellow Opel Ascona for six hundred US dollars. It was an older car that many deemed undesirable. The yellow paint was faded and a shade that was far from masculine. It was not pretty, but it did the job and I eventually developed a fondness for the thing. It was an affinity many did not understand. In fact, the more things began to take off for me at work, the more my associates made fun of my car. Germany is the home of the Autobahn and most of my coworkers drove BMW's. They took every chance they could to rib me about my junker car.

Even prospective clients gave me a hard time. They questioned if I really knew what I was talking about—and used my Ascona as evidence against me. Apparently, my advice couldn't be all that great if I had to drive that piece of junk around. Over time, I developed a counterstrategy against this attack. I began to carry a printout of some of my financial statements. I showed those who questioned my authority on the matter by saying, "If I didn't believe in this, would I be investing here?" Typically, they were able to see that my car choice was an eccentricity and not a necessity.

···

It seemed our time of trial was finally over. God had answered our prayers. In the fall of 1986, JoAnne and I were invited to attend an awards banquet for the top salesmen in the company held at a hotel in Amsterdam. To be honest, we almost didn't go. When we considered the expense of the drive, the hotel and everything else, we didn't know if we could afford it. At the same time, we didn't think we could afford *not* to go either. We finally left with the hope the company would pay for the hotel because they had invited us. That's how those things worked, right? The kids stayed with JoAnne's parents for the weekend and we drove to Amsterdam. Due to the Autobahn, the drive took significantly less time than it should have.

We showed up at the hotel and immediately felt out of place. Everything about it was draped in luxury. The parking garage even had an elevator for the cars. It was 1986; to have a car elevator was a big deal. We were unsure if the parking costs were paid for, so we parked on the street. When we later caught word that cars on the street were frequently broken into, I went out to our little yellow car, unlocked the trunk, and left it open. I figured if anyone wanted to steal it, more power to them. At least they would know there was nothing of value inside before causing damage.

We checked in at the hotel and, to our great relief, discovered the company had paid for our room. Everything was high end. We couldn't keep from staring at the extravagant paintings, furnishings and people we saw on the way to our room. Once inside, we explored the foreign territory. A large bed stood with vibrant white linens and expensive chocolates on the pillows. The bathroom was bigger than our bedroom back at the row house.

As evening approached, we dressed in our Sunday clothes and went downstairs to the awards ceremony dinner. We located our seats in the banquet room. It felt like we were children dressed in play clothes, pretending to be grown up. Everything felt so unknown. We were uncertain of the rules and therefore unsure of how to act. It was not the lifestyle either of us ever imagined being part of. All my life, I had only ever used one fork per meal. Suddenly, there were silver forks of differing sizes to the left of my crystal plate, mirrored by spoons to the right. JoAnne and I sheepishly watched others around us and mimicked their behavior to avoid embarrassing ourselves.

That night, I learned the proper way to choose which fork to use. It was simple really: you worked from the outside in. I also learned that not only does silverware have a hierarchy, but they also have a language of their own. The way silverware was placed on the plate communicated different things to the waitstaff: crossed cutlery meant you wanted more food, while a fork and knife laid together at a 45-degree angle signified you were finished. Do that—even by accident—and before you knew it, the plate was whisked away.

After dinner, the awards began. They gave expensive gifts with the awards including $15,000 Rolex watches. JoAnne and I were slightly appalled by the money that was being thrown around. It seemed like we had stepped into a different universe. We were so inexperienced that we were unaware the Lladró crystal by our place settings were party favors. The whole night was extravagant beyond our wildest dreams. When we left the hotel in our washed-out Opel Ascona, the image of Cinderella's carriage turning back into a pumpkin came to mind.

...

I have always believed buying a new car is about the worst investment you can make. The depreciation is too high; cars don't hold their value. Yet, people buy expensive cars to satisfy their pride. They don't want to be seen driving around in a cheap car. Other than saving money to invest in better ways, one major benefit to owning a car that isn't worth much is that you aren't too devastated when something happens to it.

For example, one rainy afternoon I was following someone through a traffic circle. They obviously didn't quite understand how it worked and they stopped instead of yielding. The ground was wet when I tried to stop, and I slid into the back of their car. I gave the man my insurance information and left with a dented hood that refused to latch. We did not have the money to repair the hood, so I took matters into my own hands. I borrowed a chain from a neighbor and hooked it to the front of the car. I tied the other end around a telephone pole. I used the leverage—like I had done many times on the farm—to jerk and bend the frame of the car back into place until the hood latched. Afterward, I continued to drive the car.

Another incident was more bizarre. The top salesmen in our company came from all over Europe to attend a conference at an extravagant hotel in Frankfurt. The hotel was upscale enough that you had to pay to use the parking lot. Frugal man that I was, I parked across the street instead. During a break in the conference, I looked out of the expansive high-rise windows. There was quite a bit of construction going on—cranes dotted the landscape, busily adding new skyscrapers to the skyline. Below, I could see the speck that was my yellow car. I was not the only one.

My colleagues noticed my car and began to make fun of my wheels yet again. It was obvious that I could afford a nicer car—I was at the conference, after all—why didn't

I upgrade? It was during this banter that we heard the high-pitched grating noise of sheering metal. We watched in shock as pieces of a crane across the street plummeted hundreds of feet.

One piece landed on the roof of my car! I couldn't believe it. Not only that this freak accident occurred, but that it happened as we were discussing the car. Upon inspection, there was a large dent in the roof from the debris. The funniest part of the whole thing was that the insurance company paid me 2,800 Marks for the damage, which was more than I paid for the car to begin with! I popped the dent out and continued to drive the car.

Khalid

After a series of bombings in Beirut in 1987, the United States enforced a travel ban barring citizens from traveling to Lebanon on American passports. During this turmoil, JoAnne and I were invited by our friend, Rick Roggia, to visit Israel with him. A military chaplain and high council member for our church, Rick was also serving as a stake mission president and I was one of his counselors. Due to his service as a military chaplain, he met twice a year in Salt Lake for trainings with prominent leaders from the church. We often discussed spiritual matters together and I cherished our friendship.

Despite the risks, we decided to seize the once-in-a-lifetime opportunity to visit the Holy Land. With only a week's notice, the tickets were surprisingly inexpensive—especially compared to flight prices from the States. We flew with El Al Airlines, whose planes were equipped with missile defense systems. The security at the airport was high. First, we were greeted by a tank outside. Inside, the reception was less than welcoming. We each met with interrogators who questioned our travel plans. After our interviews, we switched interviewers and went through the whole process again. Our luggage was thoroughly searched. We were then informed we had to have our bodies searched as well.

After the body searches, JoAnne leaned over to me and joked, "What? No strip searches? I'm disappointed!"

A bus with guards holding M-16s took us to the plane. Another tank sat on the tarmac. After all of that, we boarded the plane and set off to Israel.

Once in Israel, we arrived at the Paradise hotel. The pleasant hotel was newly constructed. After settling in, we started our week-long tour with Daniel Rona. Daniel was the only licensed tour guide who was also a member of the Church of Jesus Christ in Israel. Formerly a radio and TV broadcaster, he pioneered personal headsets for group members to wear during his tours, which typically consisted of fifty or more people. The headsets made it possible for everyone in these larger groups to hear him. Because of the conflicts in the area, however, we were the only three on the tour for the majority of the week. With a group so intimate, we didn't need the headphones. Due to our small number, we were able to tour places he normally could not take larger groups. We were also able to navigate the sights more quickly than planned, which left us a few hours of leisure in the evenings.

During that leisure time JoAnne and I did some exploring close to the hotel. We found a small gift shop about half a block from where we were staying. There were a few men running the shop as we entered. We learned the shop was owned by their parents. All seven sons worked at the shop. We left with a beautifully carved olive wood nativity set, but not before I was invited back for a chess match the following evening.

Over the time I spent with the brothers that week, I learned about their fascinating lives and culture. They were extremely welcoming and kind to me. I felt prompted by the Spirit to invite them to church with us before we left. In Israel, the Church of Jesus Christ of Latter-Day Saints honors the Sabbath on Saturday. To my happy surprise, they accepted my invitation.

Back at the Paradise hotel that evening, I called the local church leadership to learn where the services were held and inform them of the expected Arabic guests. To my surprise, he responded, "What? What did you do? You're not supposed to be preaching the gospel. The church could get in serious trouble for preaching the gospel."

My happiness evaporated. I didn't know I couldn't invite friends to church, but I couldn't change it now. The damage had already been done; I wasn't going to uninvite them. However, it troubled me that I had done something wrong when I was trying to do something kind. I was so upset about it that I went and knocked on Rick's door to discuss it. I shared the situation with him and sought his advice.

"Well, did you feel the Spirit?" he asked.

"Yeah, I know the Spirit directed me to share the gospel."

"Then don't worry about it," he said.

Trusting that I had felt the Spirit encouraged me to not back down. If I had done something wrong by inviting them, then perhaps this was the only invitation they would ever get. I studied the bus lines from their shop to the church building and let the brothers know which buses to take.

When Saturday rolled around, Rick, JoAnne and I sat in a small room with a handful of other families as the meeting began. We looked around after the opening hymn and prayer and felt deflated that our friends did not show up. The man leading the service had just started making announcements when the doors opened and in walked three of the brothers from the gift shop. Everyone was stunned into silence. The man up front didn't speak—long enough for me to worry what he was going to do. To my relief, the brothers took their seats and the service continued.

After the service, some members of the congregation chastised me. "Don't you realize their family members will kill them? It could really mess up their lives."

I responded that I understood that now, but I had been following the Spirit at the time.

When we got back to Germany, I located an Arabic copy of the Book of Mormon. Inside the front cover I wrote my testimony and mailed it to the gift shop.

...

In the months before the dedication of the Frankfurt temple, Rick and I worked under the direction of the stake president of the serviceman's stake, Peter Mourik. Our assignment was to oversee the presentation for the temple open house. A week and a half affair in the summer, this open house showcased to the public the beauty and spiritual nature of temples. Planning for this large of an event was the hardest I ever worked in the church — until then and since. With so many details to consider, the planning seemed endless.

We organized billboards and small presentations down the walkway to guide people through their tours. Part of our efforts included collecting enough copies of the Book of Mormon in five languages to be given to anyone who desired one.

It was the end of July. JoAnne and I had just celebrated our eighth wedding anniversary. I don't remember if we did anything special to celebrate because I was so consumed with preparing for the open house. Thankfully, the preparation paid off and the event was a great success. That week 70,000 people from all walks of life visited the Frankfurt temple prior to its dedication. A few weeks later, at the end of August, the culminating dedicatory services took place and, just like that, the Church of Jesus Christ of Latter-Day Saints now had over forty temples worldwide.

...

At the end of October that same year there was a knock on our door. Typically, I was out of the house meeting with clients in the evenings, but for some reason I was home that particular night. Not many people knew us in Germany, so we normally didn't have visitors. One of the kids ran and opened the door. To our surprise, there stood Khalid, one of the seven brothers from the gift shop in Israel. He stood on our porch nearly in tears. We learned he had been searching for us for over two months and was happy to have finally found us. He had been unable to find us for so long because he had been looking for us in Mainz, while we lived in Mainz-Kastel.

Khalid caught us up on the recent happenings in his life. He lived in Germany now, attending the University at Mainz. The university was a stepping-stone to his dream of attending school in New York City. Over the next six months Khalid periodically stopped by to visit. He wasn't interested in meeting with the missionaries, but he came to church with us on occasion. We took him in and became his family away from home. He likewise became ours.

...

The next spring, our fourth and final child—another son—was born in Germany. I had always loved the name Kai, but we couldn't exclude him from our quirky MC trend. In the end, we named him Malachi Chad and have forever called him Kai. Since we knew what to expect at the hospital this time around, we came prepared with everything but the kitchen sink. The only surprise was the Olympic trained athlete they sent to help JoAnne exercise the morning after she gave birth.

Before we knew it, Kai was nine months old. We decided to make a trip back home for the holidays. JoAnne and I boarded the plane with our four little kids and set off for the United States for the first time in over three years.

We really enjoyed time with our family after being away for so long. My parents loved being with the kids and were happy to meet Misha and Kai. When the phone rang from the other room, my dad left to answer it. He came back and said, "It's for you, Martin."

"Me?" I asked. *That's weird. How does anybody know I'm here?*

Curiosity filled me as I rose and went to the phone. I pressed the receiver to my ear and said, "Hello? This is Martin."

It was Khalid. We had given him my parents' contact information before he left Germany the year before. We figured it was the most reliable way to contact us in case we moved or changed numbers. I was happy to hear his voice. My joy grew as he explained why he was calling. He wanted to let me know he had made it to New York. He had been meeting with the sister missionaries there and was going to be baptized on Saturday.

Tears of gratitude flooded my eyes as a warm peace filled me. Our dear friend Khalid was joining the Church of Jesus Christ. My Spirit-prompted invitation to Khalid and his brothers to come to church with us eighteen months previously had born fruit—and it was good. Surely, this was what heaven must feel like.

Returning Home

We spent the Christmas season with my parents. Being back after such a long separation made us extremely homesick. We wanted to make it a permanent move. Never one to sit still, I started doing sales work for a small company in Yakima. Despite my dislike of multi-level marketing companies, an opportunity was extended to me and I took it. I thought if I could make something happen while we were on vacation, perhaps we could afford to stay.

Things rapidly began to happen. I found success the way many people do today but was revolutionary for the time; I held seminars in a rented hotel ballroom to present the products I sold. Six weeks later, I had almost fifty people in my "downline", but I could feel it was not going to last. The Spirit kept pressing me to go back to Germany. To the dismay of my parents, we re-packed our suitcases, gathered up our little family and once again traveled across the world.

We went back to our townhome in Mainz-Kastel. Shortly after our arrival, I met with President Mourik, who happily told me, "I held your spot on the high council because I knew you'd be coming back."

Unfortunately, I had to decline the assignment. We felt the Lord directing us another way.

That direction was east about two and a half hours—near Nuremberg in the city of Grafenwoehr. Grafenwoehr had a growing military presence due to new training facilities. A friend of mine owned an H&R Block office building next to military housing and rented an office to me. I continued to sell the same financial product line as before, but now I worked out of my own office. It was a risky move because I was forced to rebuild my clientele, but we felt drawn to be there.

We rented a new, two-level duplex in a tiny neighborhood in the country. We convinced the owner to rent us both the upstairs and downstairs spaces (which, of course, were kitchenless).

The church congregation there was small—about sixty-five people—and shared a building with other religions on post. I'll never forget our very first Sunday when the Spirit impressed upon me that I would be the branch president. That revelation came true within the month.

It's funny how quickly we fall into the rhythms of living. Just like that, in a new city, with a new job and church assignment, things more or less went back to how they were before.

We had been back in Germany about a month when I learned that the multi-level marketing company I worked for in Washington had continued to hold seminars in the hotel using *my* name, expecting me to foot the bill. There was no way I was going to pay those charges. After numerous calls, I finally straightened everything out so the company reserving the hotel was properly billed. I also never saw a single penny from that robust downline of mine...

...

Time marched on. Before we knew it, we had lived in Germany for five and a half years which was more than twice the time we had anticipated. JoAnne and I traveled to East Berlin numerous times over those years. We chose to travel with our military friends across the border. In those days, the Berlin Wall was highly patrolled. To cross, we passed through a series of checkpoints along a corridor that ended with Checkpoint Charlie—a small building that resembled a toll booth, parked in the middle of Friedrichstrasse—the only street that allowed foreigners behind the Berlin Wall.

There were armed guards at each checkpoint who walked around and inspected the car. They peered in to check our passports. We didn't have the same clearance as our military friends did, which meant we had to walk a portion of the checkpoint corridor with guns pointed at our backs while our friends could remain in the car. However, traveling together made the journey smoother.

Typically, we made a big trip toward the end of the year to go Christmas shopping. We traveled because the exchange rate was unheard of, in our favor. The disproportionate exchange rate was one thing to know and another thing entirely to experience. It was unreal to walk into a store and see luxurious items such as amber necklaces and fur coats for sale for what amounted to fifty dollars. We quickly learned we never had to ask for prices. Although we only brought about a hundred dollars with us, we knew it was enough to buy whatever we wanted. Once, JoAnne found a beautifully carved wooden instrument, a zither, for four dollars. It decorated our home for decades afterward.

The people there were impoverished. We felt strange buying things they had to save for months or even years to afford. We seemed to live in an entirely different world. One afternoon, JoAnne walked down the street eating a cinnamon roll with her friend who had a peach. People openly stared at them. Someone asked, "Where did you get that?"

When they replied the peach came from West Berlin, the person was obviously disappointed. The peach, it seemed, was a novelty. After that, we began to notice long lines of people at the markets. We found out they weren't waiting for anything we considered remarkable; they were waiting for fresh fruit. Whenever fruit was rumored to be in a store, people lined up, not even knowing what fruit they were waiting for. It didn't matter. They were all just hoping to make it to the front before supplies ran out.

Our seventh trip to East Berlin was perhaps the most memorable. As usual, we traveled with several military friends in a van across the border to do some shopping. As we crossed, we talked about the Wall.

"I wonder if they will ever open up this border?"

The consensus was, "Not in our lifetimes."

We spent the day shopping and treated ourselves to dinner at a fancy restaurant. As we exited the restaurant, we heard music playing and saw people dancing in the streets. It seemed extremely out of place, but we wrote it off as a possible holiday we didn't know about. We loaded ourselves into the van now packed with goods and began the drive home.

When we got to the first of the checkpoints, the intimidating guards were a fraction less stern than normal. They didn't point their guns at our backs, for instance. In fact, they didn't stop us at all. They just waved us through. We didn't know what was going on. We switched on the American forces radio and heard the glorious news. After nearly thirty years, the Berlin Wall had come down.

...

Eventually, we began to contemplate returning to America. One motivating factor was that our second son was having difficulty in school due to the language. He was being bullied. Having been bullied as a child, I knew how traumatic it was and the damage it could do. JoAnne's parents had also completed their mission and returned to Washington. They longed to have her and the babies nearby.

Another factor was financial. The American dollar had weakened significantly, which made it substantially more expensive to live in Europe than America. We cut corners where we could. We gave up half of the house and squeezed the six of us into two small bedrooms. JoAnne and I took the smaller room, which was barely large enough to walk around the sides of our queen-sized bed. The four kids shared the larger room. We put up a divider for privacy between the boys and Misha, but the situation was far from ideal.

Together, we made the decision to move JoAnne and the kids back to Washington in September of 1990. We felt that I still had work to accomplish in Germany. I continued to live and work in Germany until March of 1991. For those six months, I traveled every month to see my family. The commute was demanding—in a short period of time I traveled the world a few times over. I spent three weeks in Germany and every fourth week I traveled to Washington. JoAnne and the kids lived with her parents in Seattle during those six months. Surprisingly enough, commuting was cheaper than maintaining the family in Germany, so we made it work.

During that time, I ran into Donna and Allen Pahl, old friends from our first days in Mainz-Kastel. Donna was the one who gave us the miracle clothes for baby Misha. Since we last saw them, they had moved to the new training facilities in Grafenwoehr. They offered to rent me a room in their home, which I happily accepted. It was comforting to not come home to an empty house. During my time with them, I was finally able to repay some of their kindness by helping them manage their finances and get out of debt.

Although I spent three weeks a month without my family, I was constantly busy serving as the leader of a congregation in Germany. The calling, coupled with evenings devoid of family obligations, gave me the perfect opportunity to share the gospel. Throughout that year of leadership, and particularly the last six months, I had some of the sweetest experiences of my life. They were six months of trial—I hated being separated from my family—but the sacrifice brought forth miracles.

...

Nelson Mittock was a wiry fellow who was persistent in his comments against the church. He worked in my office building. Since we shared the building, he often overheard my conversations with others about the restored gospel. On more than one occasion, after overhearing my conversation, he left his office and caught the person on their way out to let them know what a "bunch of crap" I had fed them. He wasn't talking about any of my financial advice. Part of his antagonism against the church may have come from the fact that his wife, Sally, was a recently baptized member. Whatever the cause, he always had something negative to say.

Every once in a while, he and I got into it about the church. Despite his argumentative attitude, JoAnne and I loved Nelson. He also happened to be our next-door neighbor when we lived in the duplex. JoAnne had brought Nelson and his wife cookies on occasion.

He eventually moved to England to do financial consulting there. He had been gone for two months when I got a call I never expected. Nelson was on the other end of the line. "Martin, I want to apologize to you for the way I treated you. I'm so sorry." He paused. "And it would be an honor for me—" His voice cracked. "I've been taking the missionary discussions...I want you to fly to England and baptize me."

I was speechless. Was this Nelson? Nelson Mittock? The guy who spent a year badmouthing the gospel at every turn? Overcome, I happily agreed. We arranged the details and before I knew it, I was in England baptizing my friend and former neighbor. I saw God turn Saul into Paul.

Another miracle I witnessed that year was growth. Thanks to the help of superb counselors and members, the membership of our congregation doubled in size. We were on the brink of becoming a ward. While some of the growth was from new membership, much of it came from people coming back to church.

There were two couples at the outset of my assignment I knew I wanted to befriend. In both families, one spouse was a baptized member while the other was not. I did my best to fellowship and encourage them to seek a stronger relationship with Jesus by attending church services with us. Both of those spouses were later baptized. One of my last weeks in Germany, I witnessed both couples sealed together for eternity in the temple.

These experiences solidified within me the idea that the gospel clarifies life—it is the lens through which we gain a deeper insight into reality. I watched lives and relationships improve dramatically. It was evidence of the veracity of the restored gospel's claims. It changed people; made them better.

While I found purpose in the work, I was waiting on the Lord to send me home. A prompting from the Spirit had sent us to Germany and I was waiting for a similar confirmation that my time was complete.

I remember one Sunday morning in particular. I sat in my bedroom preparing for church services later that morning. I wrestled with my feelings for some time regarding whether to stay in Germany or leave. I lost count of how many times I had prayed regarding this same question during those six months alone. I was beginning to feel like my prayers were falling on deaf ears. I missed my family: my wife, my kids. I longed to be with them. But I wasn't sure if I had done all the Lord wanted me to do. I said another prayer in my heart and opened the scriptures.

The book fell open to the Doctrine and Covenants on page 135. I read from the top right page. Verse six read: "Therefore, verily I say unto my servant," and the Spirit prompted: *put your name there.*

I started again, "Therefore, verily I say unto my servant [Martin Van Leuven], I revoke the commission which I gave unto [you] to go unto the eastern countries".

I was overwhelmed by the message and knew I had received my answer. Without delay, I called the stake president to find someone else to fill my position. It was time for me to return home.

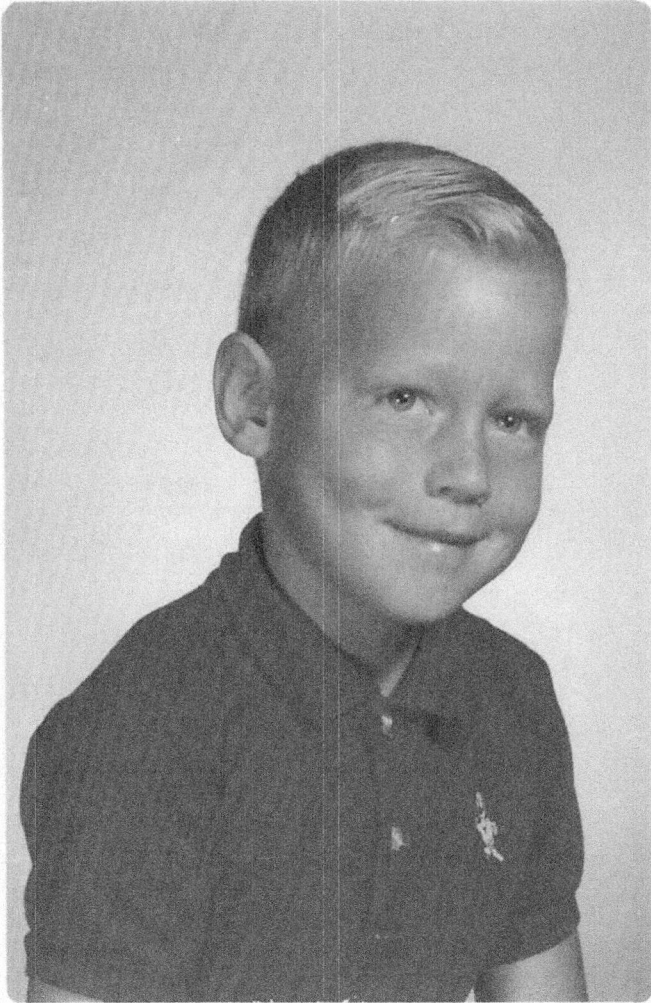

Martin Van Leuven, 8 years-old

Martin & JoAnne, Israel (1987)

Martin & JoAnne (2015)

The Van Leuven Family (2020)

Life Lessons

Create an Alternate Path

I was eleven and my sister, Kaelin, was thirteen when we got jobs picking cherries for local orchards. It almost didn't happen; the orchard owners were skeptical of our ability to keep up with the adults for the grueling ten to twelve-hour shifts. Luckily, our father was well-respected in the community and put in a good word for us. So, they took a chance on us and we were determined to prove ourselves.

It was easiest to pick the cherries while standing on the ground because as soon as I got on a ladder, I lost use of a limb. While one hand picked, I had to use my other hand to hold on to a branch for stability, thus limiting my mobility and decreasing my efficiency. After a few days of slow-moving, I brought some old jumper cables to work with me. I tied one end around my waist like a belt and let one clamp swing free. I shimmied up the ladder, eager to test out my invention. Pulling a branch close, I latched on to it with the free jumper cable. I slowly released the branch, feeling a slight pull against my waist that stabilized my position. A triumphant smile flashed across my face. I continued to pick cherries on the ladder with two free hands—giving everyone else a run for their money.

...

Returning home from Germany wasn't as easy as we thought it would be. In many ways, it felt like we were starting over, *again*. We had enough money to buy a house, but we needed a stable income, and fast.

We took up a paper route as a family while I searched for a job. It was the largest route available and spanned hundreds of houses, including our neighborhood. Such a large route required the coordinated efforts of the entire family to complete. JoAnne and I woke up around 4:00 a.m. and drove the ten miles to pick up over two hundred freshly printed papers. As I drove back to the house, JoAnne folded and tied the papers with rubber bands. If there was rain, which was often the case in western Washington, she also stuffed each paper into a plastic bag. When we got back to the house, JoAnne went inside to take care of the younger two children while Myles and Cole (then twelve and ten), sleepily lumbered out to our blue Astro van to find a large, organized pile of newspapers ready to be delivered. We weaved through the neighborhoods with the side door open and radio station 97.3 KBSG drumming out "oldies" rock and roll into the quiet morning. The boys took turns running or throwing papers from the van. Even with the boys jumping in and out, our van rarely stopped moving. We turned it into a game to see how fast we could complete the route. We got our time down to two hundred papers in under an hour. Our fastest time ever was forty-three minutes. While it was a trying period, that route produced some fond memories between me and my older boys. We all worked together to make ends meet.

Before long, I approached a friend who worked for a distinguished investing company. He knew about my financial consulting success in Germany and assured me there was a place for me at his company. While I had interviews with other companies lined up, I was excited by the prospect of working for a company as reputable as Merrill Lynch.

My first two interviews went quite well. After the second interview I received a call instructing me to arrive the next day at 6:30 a.m. for my third interview.

Early the next morning, two men escorted me to an empty back room furnished with a small desk and a corded brown phone. They motioned for me to sit. Once I did, one of the men tossed a phone book onto the desk and said, "There's the phone. We want to see you cold-call."

Keeping my composure, I replied, "Okay. I'll call. But you've got to tell me when you want your appointments scheduled."

The men exchanged looks then brushed off my question. They said they just wanted to see how I interacted with people.

"It's 6:30 in the morning. These people are going to be ticked."

The men smiled slyly at each other. They knew all too well how mad people could get that early in the morning. I imagined those unsuspecting people still warm in bed, oblivious to the impending disruption of their peace.

"We just want to see how you handle yourself in a stressful environment."

Consigned to my fate, I was determined not to proceed without purpose. I asked, "Okay. When are your openings then?"

Again, I got those knowing smiles and the "don't worry about it" response, followed by yet another round of them disregarding my request for available appointment times. I was beginning to feel like a one-track tape. But I am nothing if not persistent. If I was going to sell people investments before they'd had their morning coffee, I needed to be prepared. I told the men in suits I would not get on the phone until they provided me with available appointment times. I needed to be prepared to schedule these prospective clients to come in.

By now, I could see they were annoyed. The one who dropped the phone book said, "Look, we have been doing this for twenty years. No one has *ever* gotten an appointment. Don't worry about it. Get on the phone and start calling."

I looked him in the eye and responded, "I'm not just anybody. I'm not going to do it until you get me some times."

With a handful of times scribbled on a piece of paper, I finally got on the phone and successfully scheduled five appointments. Later in the interview process, I sat in on one of those appointments with a consultant where the client invested $100,000. Everyone was amazed. They kept singing various strains of the same tune; they had never ever seen anybody do this before. They were convinced I had guaranteed myself a position. Those interactions left me walking on clouds.

My final interview was with the regional manager in Bellevue. A dark-haired man in a suit greeted me in the waiting room. He introduced himself as Mr. Brewster.

Mentally, I don't think of myself as disabled or different, but I have always been mindful that sometimes others are uncomfortable around me because I look and walk differently. Although I knew it shouldn't, I had experienced time and time again when my physical differences hindered me from either getting a job or advancing in the workplace. The reality is that my presence made some people uneasy and, rather than have to work around me all day, they chose someone else if they could—even if I was more qualified.

Therefore, when I went to job interviews, I tried to be cognizant of this disadvantage. I even invented strategies to minimize the appearance my differences had on new people. For instance, when Mr. Brewster invited me back to his office from the waiting room, I responded, "Oh, go ahead. I'll follow you." That way, I could position myself behind him as I walked—thus being able to hide as much of my physical disability as possible.

Once in his office, I could see a stack of papers and a voice recorder sitting on his desk. "We've never seen anybody do what you've been able to pull off." He shuffled some of the papers around and looked up at me, almost incredulously, and asked, "How did you do it?"

I spent some time teaching him the secrets to my success, including some of the psychology behind my sales techniques. While technically I was the one being interviewed, I had become the teacher. Mr. Brewster had his voice recorder going and took notes furiously throughout the exchange. He was not hesitant to stop and ask me clarifying questions. At the end of the interview, he said he would call me soon.

True to his word, he called the next day. My heart accelerated as I answered the phone. It was a life changing call. Not because I got the job, but because I didn't.

Mr. Brewster told me frankly they were not going to hire me. Every word punched me in the gut. I had been tricked. Bamboozled. Taken advantage of. He had taken all of my ideas, my sales tactics. My mind filled with voices: that of my friend saying there would definitely be a place for me there; voices of other consultants telling me I would surely get the job, that I was a shoe-in. I saw the face of their new client who had made a substantial investment because of the cold call that *I* made. Then, my mind went blank. My imagined future with this company dissipated like smoke in the wind.

Not too long afterward I received another call. This time it was my friend from the company. He started the conversation sheepishly and said he was embarrassed about the whole thing and he didn't understand why they didn't hire me.

"Martin, I know you really need a job. We've been talking in the office and there are three of us who want to hire you to cold call for us."

I didn't enlighten him about the interview with Brewster or the fact I had been ripped off. Because he was my friend and hadn't been involved with what had happened, I graciously declined his offer. If it had been Brewster, I would not have been so kind. Although we could have used the money, I knew I was capable of so much more.

Feeling discouraged, JoAnne and I took a short weekend trip to raise our spirits. We took the Clipper, a small ferry, to Victoria BC. Unfortunately, it was not the peaceful retreat we had hoped it would be. The first day my leg gave out as it sometimes does, and I ended up face-planting on the pavement. My head hit hard, leaving me concussed. The entire upper left side of my face swelled to the point that I couldn't open my eye. Annoyingly, the area above my left eyebrow remained numb for a number of years afterward.

...

My experience with Brewster left a bad taste in my mouth. Bad enough that I strayed from the idea of financial consulting all together. I researched other options and approached someone I knew who invested in real estate. During our meeting, I expressed interest in his mentorship. I was dismayed when, looking me over, he informed me I would not be willing to pay the price required to be successful. Based on what he saw, he wouldn't even give me a chance.

After my failed attempts to secure a job with Merrill Lynch and despite my lack of mentorship, I trusted the Spirit to guide my steps. If there was anything muscular dystrophy had taught me, it was to get back up when I fell. I set my sights on a new path to provide for my family. The first step was to get my real estate license — mentor or not.

While we waited for things to take off with real estate, JoAnne went back to school in the evenings to receive credentials to direct a daycare center. Although she had experience watching kids in our home, she had never set foot in a daycare and didn't know the first thing about running one. With study and perseverance, she was able to finish school and start a daycare center. Through her tireless efforts, JoAnne watched our children and simultaneously provided us with a steady income while I tried to find my footing back in the States.

While JoAnne was busy running the daycare, I grew restless in my work. I had been through a slew of odd jobs that didn't seem to be taking me anywhere. Though not permanent, one of those jobs did give me some useful skills. I found the job through a flier left on our porch that advertised streamlined mortgages. I called to see if they could restructure my mortgage. Once I learned they found a way to save us money, I knew I had to learn more.

I tracked down the guy in charge of the small company and asked for a job. Unfortunately, he told me that both Snohomish and King counties were both spoken for. I remained undeterred. I told him I'd drive out to Pierce county (over an hour away) if it meant I could learn from him. Over the next five months I put over forty thousand miles on my car, but it was worth it. The streamlined mortgages were a special kind of magic. Using government programs, the company had found a way to help people refinance their homes with no upfront costs. I made a year's worth of income in just five months. Unfortunately, all good things must come to an end. Due to changes in government regulations, the program couldn't continue.

Eventually, I went back to school for an associate degree in computers. Afterward, I worked at Microsoft, then US Bank, and then a printer company called Minolta Business Solutions. I moved from job to job for a number of years—staying in each job for a year or more, but eventually I always moved on. I was never able to find a place where I belonged.

While the benefits of a corporate job were good for my family, they were not enough to ease my mind about providing for my family if anything were to happen to me. Since I was diagnosed with a disease that dramatically reduces life expectancy, I had been essentially blacklisted from most life insurance policies. Even though I inherited the disease from my grandma who lived to be ninety-seven, to a company who would have to pay out money upon my death, I was always too much of a liability. Now, I did have a small policy, but it was nothing substantial. It would not take care of JoAnne and our family if I were to die. The fear of being a burden on my wonderful wife and leaving her alone to raise our children drove me to find other ways to provide. I needed to know that I was doing everything within my power to take care of them. Burnt out by the corporate world, I eventually decided to take the leap and pursue real estate full-time. JoAnne was incredibly supportive through it all and was always hard at work running the daycare for our survival.

Take Calculated Risks

Over the years I've caught whispers of others' opinions of me. I have been marked as "crazy" by many because I take risks that others don't. What they say must be true. Otherwise, it would not be worth talking about.

For example, most wives who go away for a few days probably worry about their husbands feeding the kids properly while they are gone. Little do they know what sort of stunts JoAnne has had to put up with over the years. Like the time I surprised her with a new house.

I was researching homes around the greater Snohomish area when a house off of 92nd street in Mukilteo came on the market. After further investigation, the house was reasonably priced, in a good neighborhood, and appeared to be just the kind of deal I had been searching for. The only problem was that JoAnne was out of town attending a church youth camp for the week and deals like that don't last long. I did not want to miss this opportunity. Being the crazy person I supposedly am, I contacted the owner and made an offer. When I found out my offer had been accepted, I was thrilled. Now that we were under contract, I figured I should call JoAnne and tell her the good news. Unable to reach her, I called a friend of hers at the camp and eventually got JoAnne on the phone.

She asked why I was calling. I responded, "Hey dear, I just bought us a house. I already forged your signature; it's ours!"

I could see her face in my mind's eye—her eyebrows furrowed, eyes wide, mouth open in disbelief. "You did what?"

"Yeah. We're moving!" Then, my wonderful wife, who I owe the world to, laughed. "You're crazy."

The rest of the week passed, and JoAnne rushed home to investigate what I had gotten us in to. I took her to see the home. It was a dream of a place just over three thousand square feet with a fantastic view of the Puget Sound and Olympic mountains. It had a beautiful yard with a gazebo and hot tub. Owning a house like that seemed beyond our wildest dreams. During the walk-through, JoAnne looked at me incredulously and asked, "Martin, how are we going to pull this off?"

Using my knowledge of streamlined mortgages, I talked her through how we could structure the loan exactly right to sell our current house and cover the costs to get us into this dream home. It was a stunning home, and a good investment. I was determined to make it work. Thankfully, everything came together perfectly.

. . .

Our next family home was obtained through a more involved risk. I had my eye on a house in Lake Stevens. Right on the water, it was originally listed for over half a million dollars. I continued to watch the property and, eventually, the price dropped significantly. The deal piqued my interest and I dug into the details of the property. I wanted to find a way to make it ours, but I knew I needed leverage to make it happen.

One Sunday morning, I was headed home from church when I had the feeling that I needed to come up with a number. What were we willing to let our Mukilteo house go for? If we were going to buy the Lake House, we *had* to sell our current home—JoAnne's dream home. If we had an interested buyer for our place *before* I made an offer on the Lake House, it might be just enough leverage to make the deal work.

I turned onto 92nd street and saw a sign for an open house down the road. I turned left—having decided to check it out. I thought it could help me decide on an asking price for our home. I arrived in my suit and was greeted downstairs by the Realtor. She stayed downstairs to welcome others as I viewed the home. It was similar to ours but lacked some of the perks. For example, we had a much better view and additional amenities such as the hot tub and gazebo. When I went upstairs, I saw another couple touring the house. As I saw them, the Spirit hit me: *talk to them about buying your home.*

I approached the young couple and said, "Hey, I came here to figure out what to sell my home up the street for. I'm going to put it on the market soon. In fact, I'll give you a better deal than what they're asking for this place. If you're interested, I'll even sell it low enough that you'll have about $15,000 instant equity in the home."

They exchanged glances and the husband said, "When can we see it?"

"Oh, right now," I replied. "Just give me a couple of minutes. Come up in about five or so minutes and I'll walk you through." I gave them my address and then booked it to my car.

I barreled up the driveway, threw the car in park and headed inside. JoAnne had stayed home from church that day recovering from Lasik surgery. She was laying down with a damp rag over her eyes when I got home.

I bolted in the door to my incapacitated wife and said, "Hey honey, I think I just sold our house."

"What? This house? Are you kidding me?"

To her dismay, I said, "Nope!"

I looked at the kids and said, "Hurry up and pick up the house. Get together and pick everything up! A couple is coming up now to look at the house." My words were met with hesitation followed by frenzy. My tone told them this was no time to negotiate or complain. They got to work straightening everything up. JoAnne sat there dumbfounded, the wet rag in her hand as she blearily watched the kids run about. Perhaps she thought it was all a ploy to get the kids to clean the house. However, when she looked at me, her voice was softer this time, "You *are* kidding, aren't you?"

"No. They're on their way up here now. I just met them at an open house down the street. They are interested in buying our house. We need to sell this house in order to buy a house I found on Lake Stevens."

Now, my wife is a saint—an honest to goodness trooper. I don't know how she has put up with my antics all these years, but I'll love and appreciate her forever for it. In fact, out of all the crazy deals I've made in my life, convincing JoAnne to marry me was the best sale I ever made.

The couple arrived shortly thereafter. They peeked out back and asked, "Now does the hot tub come with the house? What about the gazebo?" I answered in the affirmative on all counts.

They stepped outside to examine the property further. JoAnne looked at me forlornly and said, "You're selling my house?"

In an effort to convince JoAnne that the move was worthwhile, I took her to see the Lake House that afternoon. Though we didn't have keys, we were able to peer through the windows and get a feel for the place. I knew it was going to need some work, but I also knew that the location was everything—located in a growing city with excellent schools, right on the water, this place was going to be *worth* something someday.

As JoAnne peered through the window, I could see she was far from convinced of my master plan. I couldn't blame her. Built in the 1920s, this house had originally been a small cabin. It had been remodeled and added on to multiple times over decades to create a hodgepodge of a structure. The inside was carpeted in multi-colored indoor/outdoor carpet. It was bad, but you almost didn't notice the carpet due to the enormous fire pit in the living room. The large circular pit filled the center of the living space and was topped with a ten-foot cone-shaped metal hood with chains. The pit was encircled by numerous ugly brown Naugahyde chairs.

JoAnne took a quick scan of the room and said, "Well, this is ridiculous Martin. It has twelve Naugahyde chairs in the living room around this meat pit that looks like a sacrificial alter."

"You're just exaggerating," I said.

"Exaggerating what?" She sounded agitated. She was probably wondering if I was the one who needed Lasik if I couldn't see how terrible this house looked.

"It doesn't have twelve chairs," I said. "It has ten."

It took a while to convince her of the Lake House's potential and what I thought it could do for our future. In order to seize that opportunity, JoAnne was going to have to sacrifice her dream home in Mukilteo for this ugly house that needed a lot of work. Never one to back away from a challenge, it was a sacrifice she was willing to make for her family.

With JoAnne on board, I needed to figure out where the rest of the money was going to come from to purchase the Lake House. After a visit to the title company, I discovered the tax parcel was a lot and a half on the lake and *another* lot and a half farther up the hill. Due to the way it was structured, it was possible to break off the top parcel and create two tax parcel IDs for the property. Armed with that knowledge, I continued to piece together my most complicated real estate deal to date.

Since we were under contract, I was able to split the parcel and sell the top portion of the property to a developer for $100,000. This was risky because he immediately began to send out surveyors to start the permitting process. That meant if I couldn't find a way to make all of the moving pieces come together, the developer would sue me for his sunk costs. Not to mention, the trouble I would be in with the couple trying to buy our current house.

The deal was a lot of work to piece together. Between the developer, our Mukilteo home, and the Lake House, we had a triple escrow closing. I was thrilled to have pulled it off, but it was bittersweet because after all of that, JoAnne's dream home was no longer ours.

Over the following years we fixed up the Lake House and made it shine. We were able to dip into the home's equity through lines of credit to finance rental homes. Purchasing the Lake House was monumental in allowing me the ability to pursue real estate full-time a few years later. The thing most people overlook about being a crazy risk-taker is that calculated risks with big potential payoffs are worth taking.

Hard Work Pays Off

My first job paid eight cents. The fall after I turned eight, my sister and I harvested potatoes in Blackfoot, Idaho. A large combine paved the way before us. Its metal fingers scored the earth and turned up potatoes. Our job was to gather the unearthed spuds.

We were each given a large wire basket that held a bushel (about eight gallons). Baskets of potatoes were then dumped into one-hundred-pound gunny sacks. Kaelin and I took turns holding the sack open while the other poured in a basketful of dirty potatoes. We walked up and down the fields gathering basket after basket to fill the brown burlap sacks. We did this hour after hour, day after day, for a number of weeks. Each one-hundred-pound sack of potatoes earned us eight cents—four cents each. Despite the dismal pay, we filled enough bags for me to purchase my very first Timex watch. It was backbreaking work, but each glance at my new watch made it worth it.

. . .

Around 2011, I acquired four duplexes in Lynnwood for a screaming deal (thanks to a great tip from my youngest son, Kai). They sat together on just over an acre and a half of land. The property was my bread and butter for years; the units were easy to rent and didn't cause me much trouble. There was no way I would ever sell them. In fact, quite the opposite was true. I was planning to increase the number of units when I was unexpectedly approached by a different opportunity.

While I was out of the house one day, there was a knock at the door. My son, Cole, answered to find a sharply dressed man in his thirties. He introduced himself as a representative for DR Horton. The developer was interested in purchasing my Lynnwood property. Cole responded, "There's no way my dad would ever sell that."

The guy nodded to acknowledge Cole, but continued, "Here's my business card, please tell him I stopped by."

When I returned home, Cole explained that someone wanted to buy my Lynnwood duplexes.

"Oh, I would never sell those."

"That's what I told the guy."

I took the business card and spent the evening pondering the proposition. I began to imagine the possibilities this could open for us. I wasn't really interested in selling them, but perhaps there were other options. For instance, I could let them develop the land and keep some of the units for myself. That would increase my profit without dealing with the headache that comes with construction. With this possibility in mind, I gave the guy a call.

We met at the Starbucks in Lake Stevens. He introduced himself and I responded, "Hey John. I just want to be up front with you, there's no way I'll ever sell them." Undeterred, John explained DR Horton's interest and made me an offer.

The number was more than double what I paid for them seven years earlier. Selling would yield a profitable return on my investment—especially when counting the rental income I had already made every month during that time.

Yet, if I kept the duplexes, they would continue to produce income for me above and beyond his offer within the next few years. I told him, "Look, this property is netting me quite a lot of revenue. For me to even consider selling, it would have to be a pretty big win for me." That was the first in a long string of meetings. Six months later, I had negotiated the offer up to nearly twice the original amount.

It was around this time that a house across the lake from ours was going up for auction. It was a house I had my eye on throughout a lengthy foreclosure process. Despite the bad roof, water-logged walls, and backed up sewage in the basement, I had a good feeling about it. I wanted to make it ours.

I approached Mike, who has been my banker for over twenty years. I said, "Mike, there is a house I want that is going up for auction in three days. You know I have that deal about to close with DR Horton. They will only let cash offers bid on this property. I plan to use the duplex money to buy the house. Will you give me a letter saying that whatever price I put on this, you will back me?" Thankfully, Mike talked with the underwriters at the bank and gave me the green light.

...

Bidding on foreclosures on the courthouse steps is nearly a thing of the past. Generally, it is not as lucrative as it once was. Years ago, when it was more profitable, I stood on those court steps every Friday.

Buying a foreclosed home is a bigger risk than typical real estate. I did research to eliminate as much of that risk as I could. For years, I combed through foreclosure listings on the Internet. I ran the numbers on over one hundred homes every week. I considered the opening bid price, the valuation on the property and a few other key figures. From there, I narrowed my list to ten- to-fifteen properties that showed promise. While I had my preferred candidates, not all remained available for the Friday auction. Owners of homes in foreclosure have the opportunity to reclaim their home before auction. Investors call this 'bouncing back'. If the properties on my short list hadn't bounced back by Wednesday, I scoped out the area and general condition of the house in person. Based on my findings, I narrowed my pool to about five homes I was willing to bid on. I prepared estimates of what I was willing to pay versus what each house would likely sell for.

The idea of buying a foreclosure for cash may have some people imagining briefcases full of crisp green dollar bills. Although I suppose that is possible, it is not the way it normally works. The process is typically handled using lines of credit—often, equity in other real estate—in the form of cashier's checks. I went to the bank to get cashier's checks every Friday morning at 9:00 a.m. The trick was to get multiple checks in varying amounts based on my estimates. I always made sure to get cashier's checks in both large and small amounts. If, for example, I bought a house for $232,000 but only had checks in increments of $10,000, I would have to pay interest on the remaining $8,000 during the week it took the paperwork to be processed and receive my change. I thoroughly prepared for each auction even though many weeks I didn't buy any houses. It was always worth finding the rare deal.

There was one auction for a house in Mukilteo I will never forget. Armed with my cashier's checks, I showed the auctioneer my funds prior to the auction. This was a rule to prevent people from bidding more than they had on hand. Afterward, I sought a place on the courthouse steps among the crowd. The opening bid for the Mukilteo house was $185,000. The bidding began and it was quickly above $200,000. At $250,000 the other bidders "fell off the books"—stopped bidding. The auction was between me and one other lady. The auctioneer increased the bid by $5,000. I was watching the facial expressions of my competitor as I continued to bid against her. The auctioneer increased the bid by $2,000, then eventually $1,000 increments. Around $265,000 she started to look nervous. Acting off of that impression, I countered every one of her bids with, "And one dollar!"

We continued this way for several more rounds. The lady bid, the auctioneer called out, "Once! Twice!" and I raised the bid by one dollar. Once the bid was $270,000, I saw her ask the man with her for money. He pulled some cash from his pocket and she raised the bid by two hundred dollars. I countered and raised by one extra dollar. Finally, she didn't have any more money to continue. After she bid her last penny, I replied to the auctioneer's call.

"And one dollar!"

I made my way to the front to sign the paperwork and pay for the property. The lady who had bid against me followed me, observing my actions to ensure that I did everything perfectly. Our bidding war had captured the attention of several people, who were also watching with interest. As I handed over the cashier's checks, I was one dollar shy. I reached into my pocket and took out my wallet. Acknowledging the audience, I pulled out a dollar bill and snapped it for dramatic effect as I said, "And one dollar!"

Everyone around me burst into laughter. Everyone except the lady I outbid, that is. Her eyes almost cut me as she scowled and stormed off.

...

Not all auctions take place on the courthouse steps. Nowadays, some foreclosure auctions happen online. This was the case for the house across Lake Stevens. I had the green light from Mike to bid, and I was not going to leave much to chance. In the days preceding the auction, I called the company handling it. After multiple calls and transfers, I was connected with the lady in charge of the auction. Thanks to her, I got an idea of what it would sell for and hints at what the reserve price was—the reserve is the amount set by the bank that releases the property. If the highest bid comes in below the reserve, the bank will retain the property to be re-auctioned later.

The auction for the house across the lake started around $480,000. It continued to climb in $25,000 increments. Once it was about $600,000, the other bidders began to fall off the books. I mean, who has that kind of money sitting around in the bank? Not many. Neither did I; but I *did* have money about to come in from DR Horton. As other bidders began to fall off, the incremental bid increases lowered. Eventually, the bid was increasing by

$5,000 increments. When I held the highest bid, I also held my breath to see what would happen next.

I received an email from the company shortly after the auction ended. I tried to hold back my excitement because I knew my bid was well below the reserve price, giving the bank the ability to retain the property. I was therefore extremely surprised when the email congratulated me and awarded me the home. I didn't know how that could be possible. My bid was well below (over one million dollars below) what the bank recently paid to buy back the property.

Within minutes, my phone rang. It was the listing agent. It turns out, the lady I had previously spoken with was on vacation. The account had passed onto someone else in her absence. This new girl had mistakenly sent the email that awarded me the home. The agent tried to tell me I had *not* been awarded the home because my bid was too low. The bank would *never* let it go for that much of a loss.

Now, someone else in my position may have been deflated to hear that. Not me. That email from the company accepting my bid had awarded me the property—it was acceptance of my offer and therefore a binding contract. I told her I didn't want to get into a legal battle, but since I had a written acceptance of my offer, the bank was legally bound to the purchase price. The bank tried a few other maneuvers to get out of the agreement, but thanks to that email, I had what I needed to enforce the contract. We closed within the month. It was a miracle.

My interest in this home was more than financial, it was personal. While researching the property, I discovered the home once belonged to Mr. Brewster's boss at Merrill Lynch. It turns out, *not* being hired there ended up being a blessing. It is what led me to real estate. My life turned out better than I could have dreamed. Not only despite my challenges, but because of them.

Let Go

When our kids were younger, we set aside one night a week as a family night. It allowed us to spend quality time together. There was often a spiritual theme to the evening. While it didn't happen every single week, the effort to make meaningful time for our family was always rewarding. I often found myself steering the conversations to how spiritual lessons could be learned from finances. For example, we often talked about the principles of stewardship, helping others and consecration. I wanted our kids to understand the importance of money. Most of all, I wanted them to learn how to manage money. If they didn't learn how to manage their money, it would be more of a burden than a blessing. Teaching them these skills while they were young would prepare them to manage the opportunities given to them in life. I also didn't want my children to grow up and lose all of their inheritance one day.

JoAnne occasionally gave me a hard time about the frequency of our financial talks during family night. I realized she may have a point when my kids began to joke about us being a mafia family—always talking about money. But even then, I continued to do it. I wanted them to be able to help not only themselves, but also others someday.

…

There comes a time in every young adult's life when they have to strike out on their own. Like a child learning to ride a bicycle, the parent cannot stabilize them forever. At some point, they have to let go. Otherwise, their child will never be able to ride on their own.

As a parent, letting go of your children may be the hardest thing you ever do—to exercise tough love for their betterment. Though difficult, this letting go is essential because it gives each child a chance to see what they are capable of.

I experienced this need to exercise tough love when my two oldest boys were in college. Both Myles and Cole were attending school at BYU in Provo, Utah. JoAnne and I were financing their education—tuition, books, rent, utilities, gasoline and more. They were riding a scholarship called Mom and Dad. Before they finished their degrees, I knew it was time for them to become more financially independent. Before they drove back to school one semester, I sat them down and we had a heart-to-heart.

I looked across the kitchen table at my two handsome boys. I was surprised time had passed so quickly. Just a few years ago it seemed, they were running around at half their height driving each other crazy. Yet, before me sat two young men. Men who I knew were on the precipice of accomplishing great things. I wanted that for them with all of my heart. I also knew they were going to need a push to get there.

I started the discussion by saying the time had come for them to be more independent. "You guys need to take this seriously," I emphasized. I outlined what JoAnne and I were willing to continue to provide and what we would no longer pay for. We would continue to pay for tuition and books on the condition they get jobs to support themselves. We would also pay for car insurance and let them continue to use our white Honda (which they named *the Hondaghini*). Nothing I said should have been a surprise to them. By all means, we were far from cutting them off.

The boys looked unsettled. They had not previously worked while attending school. I knew it was going to be a challenging adjustment, but challenges provide opportunities for growth. We pushed because we *knew* our boys could handle it. We just wanted them to know they could too.

The next morning, the boys finished packing and started the drive back to school. Late that evening, I was sitting in my bedroom looking out over the lake when I got a call. It was Myles. His voice was upset, and he said, "Dad, the Hondaghini broke down and we need help."

He said they were stuck on the side of the road near Lehi, several miles north of Provo.

Seeing this as a key teaching opportunity, I said, "Oh, okay. Figure it out." and I hung up the phone.

Immediately, I received a second call. Myles again.

"Hey Dad. Did we get disconnected? What happened?"

I responded, "Hey, remember the talk I had with you before you left? You know, about how the car is your responsibility? I'll let you use it and I'll even pay the insurance, but the gas and the maintenance are your responsibility."

He was silent for a second. Then I heard, "Dad, we just drove it down here. You *just* gave it to us, and it broke down!"

I knew I had to let go and let them realize they could balance on their own without my hand guiding them. I said, "That was the deal, figure it out." I hung up. Immediately, I began to cry.

JoAnne had heard my end of the conversation and how tough I was on the boys. I had her full support, but when I hung up and started crying like a baby, she gave me a look that said, *are you insane?*

Age has softened me, especially anything involving my kids. It literally hurt me to the point of tears to be so tough on my boys. It reminded me of when my dad would say, "This is going to hurt me more than it hurts you." As a parent, I now felt what he meant.

An hour or so later, my phone rang again. The boys had towed the Hondaghini to a nearby shop and had a mechanic look it over. They said, "We did the research, Dad. The car has been towed and it's going to cost $300 to fix it. Can you give us the credit card information?"

Emboldened, I said, "No. You're not listening to me. *You* have to pay for your car."

"But Dad, after we pay for the car, we won't have enough money to buy our books and everything."

Before I lost my edge, I said, "Well, figure it out." *Click.*

It's so hard to give tough love, I lamented as I began to sob afresh.

A while later, I received their final call. Much more humbly than I had previously heard, they admitted, "Dad, we just don't have the money."

Well, they are my boys, and I love them. I responded with a compromise. I *loaned* them the money to fix the car, but they were going to have to pay me back. As a sign of good faith, I gave them one week to find jobs.

Within the week I received calls from both my boys. They had both been hired by Dish Network as door-to-door salesmen—100% commission jobs with no hourly pay. Having been in sales for a number of years myself, I thought, *Oh, that's a tough way to go.* But a job was a job, and I knew if they persevered when things got tough, they would succeed. I celebrated with them; they had met my stipulation and secured jobs.

They spent the next week knocking doors, but neither one made any sales. They called me extremely frustrated that things weren't working out. I gave them each tailored advice on how to approach selling based on their personalities and asked them to let me know how it went. On Saturday, they each had a few sales which gave them hope.

The next Saturday, Cole found what he thought was a promising area. He has a natural gift for research and strategy. Both he and Myles hit the pavement in that area. After a long day, they excitedly called to report that one of them made ten sales and the other eleven, which gave them each a significant commission. It was the confidence boost they needed to stick with it and find further success over the following years.

That was a turning point for my older boys. They learned they didn't need to depend on JoAnne and me as they had been, they were ready to take off the training wheels and ride. They didn't realize they could do it on their own until they looked back and saw we had already let go.

Never Give Up

I loved sports growing up, but my disease forced me to abandon most physical activity as a teenager. When I was diagnosed, it felt like part of me died; I have mourned the loss throughout my life. However, a small part of me felt reborn when my boys took up wrestling. Myles and Cole both wrestled in school. In fact, Lake Stevens' renowned wrestling program was part of our motivation to move there. Following in his older brothers' footsteps, Kai started wrestling young. He joined a wresting club in Everett before he was old enough to wrestle for school.

Something you should know about Kai; he has always been an extremely driven person. Even as a small child, he did all he could to keep up with brothers five and eight years older than him. When I first took him to wrestle and he got beat by the more experienced kids, I knew if he persevered, he would find success. But it was still heartbreaking as he cried in the car on the way home from practice.

No one likes being beaten—much less, beaten up— least of all, Kai. Yet it happened over and over. During those first weeks when he wanted to give up, I said, "Kai, even though you're getting beat up, you're learning. Someday, you are going to be able to give the punishment. You have to take it before you can dish it out."

Thankfully, he stuck with it. Before he left the club for high school wrestling, we traveled to tournaments across the nation together. The crowning moment was when— wrestling in one of the toughest weight classes in Washington State his senior year—Kai won the state championship.

. . .

Our daughter Misha received her first drivers permit when she was eighteen. Misha enjoyed going places with JoAnne and therefore didn't have a pressing desire to learn to drive herself. Because of this, teaching her to drive was a lengthy process.

Like most people, we started in an empty parking lot. It was a struggle at first, as she confused the brake and gas pedals. Little by little, we worked our way onto the streets. Unfortunately, the stimulation proved to be overwhelming. Many nights, the stream of changing information flustered Misha and caused us to end our driving practice sooner than intended. On occasion, she had to pull over and let me drive home to ensure we made it in one piece. Nevertheless, we went driving multiple times a week to help her get the practice she needed. Thinking back, it would have helped to have a

167

brake on the passenger side of the car like a driving instructor.

Months turned into years and we continued to practice. Each time we had to renew her permit, I could tell she felt impatient with herself and the process. I couldn't blame her.

As she prepared for her driving test, we took extra care to drive around neighborhoods in Everett where the test would take place. Typically, we drove around slower areas where there were less people. We planned driving practice to avoid rush hour and most commuters, but I knew she needed more experience with realistic conditions as well.

One day I had her turn onto Evergreen Way—an artery street in the city. We practiced thinking ahead—if she wanted to turn right at the upcoming light, she was going to have to merge sooner rather than later. However, her insecurity with merging manifested itself in serpentine maneuvers down the lane. Suddenly, blue and red lights filled the car from behind. A wave of dread washed over me. I instructed Misha to pull to the side of the road and put the car in park.

Being pulled over is never a fun experience, but it completely unnerved Misha. She was extremely agitated by the time the officer appeared at her window. Leaning forward, I tried to explain to him that I was her dad, and we were practicing driving. He told me he pulled her over because he thought she was intoxicated.

It was so unexpected; I began to chuckle. Unfortunately, this annoyed the cop.

Putting his hand on his weapon, he said, "Show me your hands!"

"What?" I asked, confused.

"Show me your hands!"

Looking down, I noticed my hands had fallen limply off my lap when I leaned forward to talk to him.

"What's down there under your seat?" He must have thought I was reaching for a weapon. Exposing my palms, I explained I had no strength in my arms and was just resting them there. I was surprised by how quickly the situation had turned. Misha and I were the least threatening pair I could think of. After talking a bit more, we reached the consensus that Misha was not drunk, and I was not a threat. Thankfully, the officer let us go on our way.

...

It took several years of practice before Misha was ready to take her driving test. The last time we went to renew her permit, we practically had to beg the person behind the desk to give it to her. It was her fourth and final permit; she had to make it count.

The day Misha got her license was a dream fulfilled. I was incredibly proud of her. Whenever I think of that day, I get emotional. After years of anxiety, frustration, anger, tears, and near accidents, we were victorious at last.

Keep Your Word

Traditions can unify families. For example, some families take Sunday walks in the park. Others look at Christmas lights every year. In our family, we cruised the streets—driving for dollars—in my white Ford Ranger on the lookout for shabby properties to buy. It was on one of those drives that Kai found his first property.

JoAnne, Kai and I were sardined in the cab of the truck. We were hunting for the diamond in the rough of Everett. We turned left on Hoyt and drove slowly past a large house. I almost didn't see it through the expansive pine trees. Kai pointed through the forest, and said, "Dad, we are going to buy that place."

Closer inspection revealed the home was a spacious two-level duplex. Each floor was about 1,500 square feet. Bay windows formed a turret up the left side. There was also a glass-enclosed porch on the second level that provided rain cover for the two front doors beneath it. We weren't surprised to learn the neighbors called it the "haunted house"—it was clear the exterior hadn't seen a paintbrush in decades. With some TLC however, the property could show promise.

When our kids were small, JoAnne and I started depositing money every month into savings accounts for each of them. By the time they graduated from high school, there was a nice nest egg to help them get their feet on the ground. The primary intent of those funds was to pay for a mission, but it could also be used to pay for college. When we found the house on Hoyt, Kai proposed using income from his part-time job, along with some of the nest-egg funds, to buy into the property. Together, we planned to fix it up, rent it out and split the profits. Since he was using money that had been earmarked for a mission, I agreed to the arrangement on the condition that he use the proceeds from the property to fund his missionary service. He agreed.

Kai tracked down the property owner and arranged a meeting. He was an older gentleman named Jim. We met him at his small cabin in the woods. We introduced ourselves and spoke of our interest in purchasing the Hoyt house. He had purchased the property decades ago and had since lost interest in managing it. Jim agreed to sell us the tired home and we negotiated the terms at a table outside the cabin. He even offered to help us cut down the enormous pines in front of the house after closing.

The Hoyt house needed extensive remodeling. Peeled paint aside, the house had zero curb appeal—it wasn't even visible from the street! Thankfully, Jim made good on his offer and aided us in felling the seventy-five-foot trees.

As with any remodel, there were many large decisions to be made. One decision was whether to make a big project even bigger. We were already working with two units that had endured years of use and neglect from renters. However, the expansive cathedral ceilings in the attic tempted us to convert the exposed beams into an additional 1,000 square feet of living space. It was a temptation we couldn't resist. The addition made this house a real monster at about 4,000 square feet. We were thrilled by the challenge.

A narrow alley ran behind the house. Stairs hugged the side of two detached garages and descended from the alley into the yard. Across the yard, two flights of stairs led up to the second story porch. Once inside, on the other side of the house, a steep staircase led to the attic. In total, there were three flights of stairs from the garage to the attic.

A consequence of finishing off the attic space was having to move materials up there. The house was tall, and the steep staircases were not for the faint of heart. We needed over one hundred sheets of heavy duty 5/8-inch sheet rock moved up there. At about one hundred stairs a trip, it was no easy task. Unfortunately, I was not able to help with that kind of work.

A friend came to help Kai and JoAnne move the heavy sheets. They worked in a rotating system: each person took two trips carrying one end of a board and rested every third board. JoAnne is a workhorse and often does more than her share. Such was the case that day. She frequently skipped her turn to rest. She said things like, "Oh, just go ahead and rest," and, "I'll take the next one too." She preferred to work as hard and as quickly as possible. The friend who helped move the sheet rock commented, "Man, your wife's putting me to shame."

...

One afternoon Kai was on a ladder with a Sawzall. Sawdust spewed onto the newly laid attic floor. When I walked across the room, my feet slid out from under me. I fell on the floor with my legs forced into the splits. I cried out as pain shot up from my right leg. Kai looked down at me from the ladder. I tried to move but I couldn't. Kai climbed down the ladder, helped me reposition, and then we laughed together in shock.

"What are we going to do?"

Kai suggested an ambulance. I declined. I hate ambulances and could not stand the thought of spending so much money on a short ride across town. We had to get me there on our own. I told Kai, "Just shove my leg over—parallel to my other leg."

174

My leg looked like a stuffed denim sausage. I laid sweating on the floor and felt the shock begin to take over. Kai rolled me onto my left side and used my left leg as a brace for my right. Then, like a board, he tipped me upright onto my feet.

"You gotta get me on your shoulder."

Kai has never been a big kid, but between club wrestling and high school, he wrestled nearly year-round. Kai nodded and squatted down to dead lift me lengthwise along his shoulders. Although I was heavier than him, he didn't falter. Not only did he have to carry my weight, but Kai also had to support my injured leg with his arm so that it remained straight. Otherwise, I probably would have passed out from the pain. Once we were situated, he began our decent.

He turned sideways and made his way down the narrow staircase from the attic to the second floor. He then carried me across the length of the house and outside. Next, we descended two flights of stairs and crossed the yard. I don't know how he did it, but he then carried me *up* the stairs and into the alley—never failing to support my injured leg.

What a sight we must have been. He put me down in the alley. I leaned against a pole while he ran to the front to get the pickup. Our entrance didn't go unnoticed. Two ladies walking down the alley stopped when they saw me. One of the women asked, "Are you alright?"

"No. I really messed up my leg. My son went to go get the pickup."

"Why don't you call an ambulance?" she asked.

Shaking my head, I replied, "Nah. My son can take me. But I may need help getting into the pickup."

She nodded but seemed ready to press the ambulance issue as Kai rounded the corner in the truck. It was quickly determined I was unable to sit in the truck cab. Like a woman in a tight dress, I couldn't bend into a seated position. Instead, Kai unlatched the tailgate. The women helped Kai lift me and I fell like a board into the back of the pickup. I scooted toward the cab as Kai shut the tailgate and thanked the ladies for their help.

The ride across town in the back of the pickup was less than desirable for someone who was severely injured, but we made it. Kai parked the truck in front of emergency and went to get help. When the attendant came out of the hospital and saw the empty cab he asked in bewilderment, "Where is he?"

"In the bed of the truck."

A few seconds later the attendant's head popped into my line of sight. I breathed a sigh of relief. We had made it.

The fall did quite a number on my right leg. Muscles, ligaments, tendons—you name it, I tore it. The doctor wanted to keep me in the hospital with the prospect of taking me into surgery. That wasn't going to work for me. JoAnne had planned a surprise get-away to Las Vegas for my birthday. Our flight left that afternoon, and I was going to catch it—even if I had to hobble the whole way. Instead of surgery, I asked for some Tylenol and to be discharged.

Due to my injury, we rented a scooter (for the first time in my life) to help me maneuver around the Vegas Strip. We had so much fun with that thing. It felt like we were kids again. JoAnne stood on the back of the scooter holding onto my shoulders while I wheeled us around in style. Everyone around us got a big kick out of it. While in Vegas, we went to an Aladdin show and a Beatles concert. All these years later, I have a picture of us from that trip hung by my desk.

...

Within the year, I got a call from Kai who was attending college at BYU-Idaho. He announced he was going to marry his girlfriend, Allison. While I was happy for him, my response was guarded. I reminded him he still needed to serve a two-year mission like he promised. He told me he was going to get married instead of serving a mission.

I knew it must have been difficult for him to call me that day. It never feels good to tell a parent something you know will disappoint them. Yet, considering what my mission did for me, I knew his could likewise cement

177

the gospel foundation of his life. It was a life-changing opportunity I didn't want him to miss. I knew the only way he would listen to me was to hold him to his word. So, that's the approach I took.

"When we bought the house together, you made the commitment to serve a mission. That was the deal. You were going to use that money to pay for your mission. If you don't go, the house is no longer yours."

To say Kai was upset would be an understatement. He didn't think he should be held to the terms of our agreement. Things had changed since then. He wanted to forgo the mission and get married now—and also keep his stake in the house. Unfortunately for him, my answer was no. I would not let him break his commitment and keep the house.

After our conversation I grabbed some papers and went to my car. JoAnne asked what I was doing. I responded that I was going to Rexburg to talk to Kai. I wanted him to know I was serious. The paperwork was for him to sign his portion of the Hoyt house over to me.

JoAnne stared at me. "You're doing *what*?"

"He says he's not going on a mission. He's going to get married instead. The agreement he made when we bought that house was that he was going to serve a mission. If he breaks that agreement, he's no longer an owner of that house."

JoAnne raised her eyebrows and looked at me like I was crazy. Perhaps I was.

I drove for twelve hours straight. When I finally reached Kai's apartment building, I knocked on the door, paperwork in hand. Kai could not believe I had driven all that way. His roommates were in the living room behind him, so I asked if we could talk outside.

"You know why I'm here. You have decided to get married now, so you are no longer an owner of this property." I continued, "I have the quick claim deed here. I am going to need you to sign the house over to me. You will no longer have claim on it because you are not going on a mission. I want you to sign it right now." I put the paperwork down on the hood of the car.

Oh man, was he mad—absolutely furious. But I refused to be swayed. "Hey, that was our commitment, our agreement. If you break it, the deal is void."

A heated discussion ensued. I stood my ground until he signed the paper. Without anything else to discuss in our emotional state, I turned to leave. Before I closed the door, I turned back and looked at my son. He was obviously fighting an internal battle. It broke my heart, but I knew this was for his good. More compassionately than I had been since I arrived, I said, "You know, if you change your mind and go on a mission, I won't record your signature on this." (The signature was not valid until it was recorded at the Snohomish County office.) If he fulfilled his terms of our agreement, I would make good on mine. The choice was his.

By this time, it was pretty late, but I decided to stop by and see Myles' in-laws, who lived close by, on my way out of town because, how often was I in Rexburg? Instead of staying the night however, I started to drive back home. A few hours into my return journey, Kai called me. He wanted to meet up and discuss things further. I told him there was nothing more to talk about. I was already in Boise, on my way home.

"You're where?"

"I'm in Boise. I had to go back home. I have things to do."

This sent a message bigger than words could have. He knew how serious I must have been to drive all the way there and back just for his signature.

Perhaps it wasn't the best way to help my son decide to serve a mission, but this was bigger than a mission. He made me a commitment—him serving a mission was a material part of our partnership. If he was going to back out of that commitment, I would exercise my right to cancel our contract. I wanted my son to learn the power of giving someone your word.

He called a few days later. "Dad, I'm going on a mission."

...

Kai served an honorable mission, returned home, and married his sweetheart, Allison.

Weather the Storm

My extended family on my mother's side had a reunion in the early 2000s. Because of the strain of muscular dystrophy throughout my family, a specialist who studied the disease made an appearance. He spent the day collecting DNA samples from my family members. Whenever I saw him approaching with his swab kit, I headed in the opposite direction. For some reason, allowing myself to be tested felt wrong to me. Deep down, I relied on my faith in the healing blessing I received so long ago. I did not want to do anything to seem ungrateful to God.

...

In fact, quite the opposite was true. I wanted to live my life as a tribute to the Lord. As a testament to this, JoAnne and I have spent the last decade serving in the temple on Friday nights. We love volunteering, yet it has not always been easy to make it there. At times, I have had to push through physical pain to get to the temple. On these occasions, I give myself pep talks: *just make it to the doors of the temple.* I trust if I make it there, it will be worth it. JoAnne and I serve to thank the Lord for our life together. We want to give Him everything we have in return for it.

Thankfully, we continue to serve even as my ability to get around declines. Unfortunately, once in a while, my right foot decides to be "lazy" and drops as I walk. When this happens, I know I am going to fall. I can't prevent it. The muscle to lift my foot up is not there anymore.

Falling poses major problems now that I am getting older. Mainly, because I cannot get up by myself anymore. Most people have either some upper body strength or some lower body strength and, sometimes, both. I have neither. It is extremely humbling to be at the mercy of gravity in such situations. In all the years we have volunteered at the temple, I have only fallen once. I was walking toward the elevator when my leg unexpectedly gave out. Without hesitation, the men around me popped me back onto my feet and we went about our business.

There is a good amount of walking required to aid others through their temple experience. Due to this, those who need assistance walking are discouraged from serving as a temple worker. Therefore, I was saddened when I finally had to buy a motorized scooter to help me get around. To my delight, however, I was given permission to use my scooter in the temple (for now).

. . .

Being healed as a young missionary cemented the foundation of my faith. It gave me an experience to cling to whenever life became difficult and my faith felt fragile. Yet, being healed did not mean God took away the damage that had already been done. I still have all the signs of muscular dystrophy. My muscles are atrophied — most noticeably on the right side of my body. My biceps are so far gone I have spent nearly my entire life unable to raise either arm above my head.

One of the side effects of atrophied muscles is pain. Simply walking around strains my muscles to the point that I experience charley horses whenever I lay down at night. To an outside observer, I may appear to be an insomniac, but it is not restlessness that keeps me awake, it is pain. Regardless of the pain, I have been wary of narcotic medication throughout my life. For me, it dulled the pain, but it also dulled my sensitivity to the Spirit. Since I have needed the guidance of the Spirit every day of my life, I avoid strong medication. Instead, I have a standing massage therapy appointment each week. The process is excruciating but necessary for me to function. The pain will only get worse as I continue to age, so I do my best to push through it and go on living.

. . .

I am forever thankful for my wife. Looking back through our life together, I cannot believe how far we have come. JoAnne has been my greatest partner and I have likewise tried to be hers. I am convinced there is not a problem she cannot fix. No matter the situation, she always jumps in with both feet.

Two years ago, I was home alone when I fell and cracked my chin open. I called JoAnne but she was stuck at the daycare for some time before she could come home to help me. My chin was bleeding quite a bit as I laid there. The blood formed a warm, sticky pool on the wood floor. Try as I might, I could not get up. Thankfully, after considerable effort, I was able to roll onto my back. Gravity kept me pinned to the floor until JoAnne got home to help me.

I know it has not always been easy for me, but it has not been easy for her either. She does a tremendous amount to help me every day. I have been trying to be more cautious and take it easier lately for both of our sakes. One way she helped me was by encouraging me to seek better medical attention.

We live about thirty miles north of Seattle. Therefore, it was not surprising when JoAnne began encouraging me to see Dr. Weiss—a renowned neurologist specializing in muscular dystrophy—at the University of Washington. She thought he could help me manage my muscle atrophy and perhaps even teach us some new lifting techniques to pick me up after I fell. For the first year, I declined. I found one excuse after another to put it off. Thankfully, she persisted.

As it became more difficult to get around, I began to be softened by her reasoning. Maybe he *could* help me. I finally consented to see him. Eventually, the day of my appointment arrived. As I had feared, Dr. Weiss wanted to do some testing. As with previous offers for muscular dystrophy testing, I turned him down. However, he discovered some issues with my heart and scheduled a follow-up appointment. Due to the other problems I was experiencing, I gave in and agreed to have some testing done.

A month passed without any results. When another month went by without hearing anything, I finally called the office to check in. I was transferred to a nurse who answered the phone with a hesitant voice. She seemed unsure of how to explain the results to me. They ran over twenty-eight tests on my samples. Each test searched for a different strand of muscular dystrophy. They did multiple variation tests to double check the results. They could not understand it. My body showed obvious signs of muscular dystrophy, but my DNA showed *no* signs of the disease. I no longer had muscular dystrophy.

A wave of emotion washed over me with a force. I felt both humbled and triumphant. I believed they were not going to find the disease in my samples. Yet, to hear confirmation of something I held onto in faith for nearly forty years was overwhelming. My faith was my lifeline when my symptoms were too much to bear. That belief gave me the strength to keep going. When I received the negative results, something solidified within me. I needed my faith no longer because I finally knew for sure. Yes, the signs remained; my muscles were gone. They would not come back. Yet, God worked a mighty miracle in me. I believed it the moment it happened in that hotel room over forty years ago.

...

As I look back over my life, I am reminded of a parable taught by Jesus about two men—one was foolish, and one was wise. One man heard the teachings of Christ but did not follow them. Jesus compared him to a foolish man who built his house on the sand. When the rains descended, and the floods came, and the storms of life beat upon the house, it fell. The other man—whom Jesus referred to as wise—followed His teachings and built his house upon a sure foundation. When the same rains descended, and the floods came, and the storms of life beat upon the house, it did not fall.

Epilogue

The greatest joy of any parent is to see who their children grow up to be. Our children have been the crowning jewels of our life together. Our story would not be complete without them. We want to publicly acknowledge how proud we are of each of them.

Myles and his wife Laura have five wonderful children, Olivia, Sophia, Dice, Eliza, and Jack. Myles was diligent and made sacrifices to obtain a higher education. After undergraduate studies, he earned a dual J.D./M.B.A. degree with honors. After college, Myles excelled in his field working for a reputable software company. He has always made friends easily and reaches out to others. Myles is an extremely spiritual man and a leader who follows inspiration for his family. He is all heart.

Cole likewise pursued higher education and earned an MBA. He has a keen sense of adventure and has traveled to forty-seven countries. Cole lives a healthy lifestyle and is a great cook. A true entrepreneur at heart, these passions led him to develop an all-natural supplement to help others with anxiety called Zenium. Cole is also well-read. His interests include politics and society. Cole is kind and has a personal relationship with

God. We often feel that the Lord answers Cole's prayers before anyone else's.

Misha is a devoted wife to her husband Calvin. She is a kind and supportive friend, sister, and aunt. Misha has an amazing memory. She spends her time thinking of others and finding ways to show her love. She does things in her own time and she does them well. Misha is unconcerned about her image and focuses on loving her family. She and Calvin are expecting their first child. We know Misha's nurturing personality will make her a great mother.

Kai is the hardest worker we have ever known. He took the small seeds of real estate knowledge we gave him and turned it into an empire through diligent effort. Kai is committed to his wife, Allison, and their two beautiful children Beck and Cozi. He spends his time being productive and teaching his children the value of education and hard work. Kai is a strong priesthood leader in his home. He is a man of faith and integrity. As far as living the gospel of Jesus Christ is concerned, Kai is 100%, all in.

To our children and grandchildren, the legacy of our faith lives on through you.

Acknowledgments

Martin and JoAnne, thank you for letting me capture part of your life story in words; it has been an honor.

I thank my husband, Kevin, who has made sacrifices and encouraged me throughout the lengthy process of achieving this dream.

Of course, this book would not have been possible without one of my personal heroes, Daniel Alderson. You not only taught me how to write, but you also helped me believe in myself. Thank you.

A huge thank you also goes to Jenny Harris, Paige Jacobson, and Myles Van Leuven for being insightful beta readers and sounding boards as I worked to piece this narrative together. I also want to thank Cole Van Leuven for his help with cover design and marketing. Thank you, Debbie Burns, for letting me pick your brain about the publishing process. Thank you, Sara Sutton, for editing.

I also want to thank my family and friends for their interest, encouragement, and support in my writing endeavors. There have been many times when your interest has kept me from giving up. Thank you.

Above all, I want to thank God for answering my prayers each time I sat down to write. I could not have done it without Him.

About the Author

Taylor Birch earned a bachelor's degree in sociology from Brigham Young University. She lives in Washington State with her husband and two daughters.

Visit her website at www.taylormbirch.com.

Made in the USA
Coppell, TX
02 June 2021